ENERGY POLICY: ISSUES, ACTIONS AND CONSEQUENCES

ENERGY POLICY: ISSUES, ACTIONS AND CONSEQUENCES

QUENTIN V. HARRIS
EDITOR

Nova Science Publishers, Inc.
New York

For permission to use material from this book please contact us:
Telephone 631-231-7269; Fax 631-231-8175
Web Site: http://www.novapublishers.com

Library of Congress Cataloging-in-Publication Data

Available upon request

ISBN: 978-1-60692-225-5

Published by Nova Science Publishers, Inc. ✝ New York

CONTENTS

PREFACE

Energy policy is the manner in which a given entity (often governmental) has decided to address issues of energy development including energy production, distribution and consumption. The attributes of energy policy may include legislation, international treaties, incentives to investment, guidelines for energy conservation, taxation and other public policy techniques. This new book explores important issues related to this set of problems which seems to define the 21st century to date.

Chapter 1 - Historically, U.S. federal energy tax policy promoted the supply of oil and gas. However, the 1970s witnessed (1) a significant cutback in the oil and gas industry's tax preferences, (2) the imposition of new excise taxes on oil, and (3) the introduction of numerous tax preferences for energy conservation, the development of alternative fuels, and the commercialization of the technologies for producing these fuels (renewables such as solar, wind, and biomass, and nonconventional fossil fuels such as shale oil and coalbed methane).

Chapter 2 - Energy efficiency issues include research and development (R&D) priorities, funding for climate-related efficiency programs, implementation of equipment efficiency standards, regulation of vehicle fuel efficiency, and electricity industry ratemaking for energy efficiency profitability. The Bush Administration has proposed an Advanced Energy Initiative (AEI) to accelerate hydrogen programs. For the Department of Energy's (DOE's) energy efficiency R&D programs, the Administration seeks \$484.7 million, with increases for Hydrogen and Hybrid/Electric Propulsion. The request would cut \$74.8 million from the Weatherization Program and eliminate controversial funding earmarks. The House-passed version of the FY2007 Energy and Water Appropriations Bill (H.R. 5427) would fund AEI and cut earmarks. The Senate Appropriations Committee has also approved AEI funding and would cut earmarks even further than the House.

Chapter 3 - The Energy Independence and Security Act (P.L. 110-140, H.R. 6) is an omnibus energy policy law that consists mainly of provisions designed to increase energy efficiency and the availability of renewable energy. This report describes the key provisions of the enacted law, summarizes the legislative action on H.R. 6, and provides a summary of the provisions under each of the titles in the law.

Chapter 4 - With recent high energy prices and the passage of major energy legislation in 2005 (P.L. 109-58) and 2007 (P.L. 110-140), there is ongoing congressional interest in promoting alternatives to petroleum fuels. Biofuels — transportation fuels produced from plants and other organic materials — are of particular interest.

Chapter 5 - Carbon is stored in the atmosphere, in the oceans, in vegetation, and in soils on the land surface. Huge quantities of carbon are actively exchanged between the atmosphere and the other storage pools of carbon. The exchange, or flux, of carbon between the atmosphere, oceans, and land surface is called the carbon cycle. In sheer magnitude, human activities contribute a relatively small amount of carbon, primarily as carbon dioxide (CO_2), to the global carbon cycle. Burning fossil fuels, for example, adds less than 5% to the total amount of CO_2 released from the oceans and land surface to the atmosphere each year. If humans add only a small amount of CO_2 to the atmosphere each year, why is that contribution important to global climate change?

In: Energy Policy: Issues, Actions and Consequences
Editor: Quentin V. Harris
ISBN 978-1-60692-225-5

Chapter 1

ENERGY TAX POLICY: HISTORY AND CURRENT ISSUES*

Salvatore Lazzari

ABSTRACT

Historically, U.S. federal energy tax policy promoted the supply of oil and gas. However, the 1970s witnessed (1) a significant cutback in the oil and gas industry's tax preferences, (2) the imposition of new excise taxes on oil, and (3) the introduction of numerous tax preferences for energy conservation, the development of alternative fuels, and the commercialization of the technologies for producing these fuels (renewables such as solar, wind, and biomass, and nonconventional fossil fuels such as shale oil and coalbed methane).

The Reagan Administration, using a free-market approach, advocated repeal of the windfall profit tax on oil and the repeal or phase-out of most energy tax preferences — for oil and gas, as well as alternative fuels. Due to the combined effects of the Economic Recovery Tax Act and the energy tax subsidies that had not been repealed, which together created negative effective tax rates in some cases, the actual energy tax policy differed from the stated policy. The George H. W. Bush and Bill Clinton years witnessed a return to a much more activist energy tax policy, with an emphasis on energy conservation and alternative fuels. While the original aim was to reduce demand for imported oil, energy tax policy was also increasingly viewed as a tool for achieving environmental and fiscal objectives. The Clinton Administration's energy tax policy emphasized the environmental benefits of reducing greenhouse gases and global climate change, but it will also be remembered for its failed proposal to enact a broadly based energy tax on Btus (British thermal units) and its 1993 across-the-board increase in motor fuels taxes of 4.3¢/gallon.

The 109th Congress enacted the Energy Policy Act of 2005 (P.L. 109-58), signed by President Bush on August 8, 2005, provided a net energy tax cut of $11.5 billion ($14.5 billion gross energy tax cuts, less $3 billion of energy tax increases) for fossil fuels and electricity, as well as for energy efficiency, and for several types of alternative and renewable resources, such as solar and geothermal. The Tax Relief and Health Care Act

* This is an edited, excerpted and augmented edition of a CRS Report RL33578, dated June 10, 2008 publication.

of 2006 (P.L. 109-432), enacted in December 2006, provided for one-year extensions of these provisions. The current energy tax structure favors tax incentives for alternative and renewable fuels supply relative to energy from conventional fossil fuels, and this posture was accentuated under the Energy Policy Act of 2005.

At this writing, congressional action is focusing on expansion and liberalizations of energy tax subsidies, as well as extension of expired or about-to-expire energy tax provisions in H.R. 6049, which was approved by the House on May 21. In the Senate, energy tax action is being taken on essentially two different versions of tax extenders and energy tax provisions — a modified version of the Senate's tax extenders bill, S. 2886, and a Republican bill, S. 3089. Also Senate Democratic leaders introduced S. 3044, the Consumer-First Energy Act, which would repeal tax code provisions that are advantageous to the oil and gas industry and impose a windfall profits tax on that industry. Finally, the recently enacted farm bill (P.L. 110-234) also expands and reforms several energy tax provisions — all tax subsidies for renewable and alternative fuels from crops — but also includes a 6¢ reduction in the excise tax credit for fuel ethanol.

INTRODUCTION

Energy tax policy involves the use of the government's main fiscal instruments — taxes (financial disincentives) and tax subsidies (or incentives) — to alter the allocation or configuration of energy resources. In theory, energy taxes and subsidies, like tax policy instruments in general, are intended either to correct a problem or distortion in the energy markets or to achieve some social, economic (efficiency, equity, or even macroeconomic), environmental, or fiscal objective. In practice, however, energy tax policy in the United States is made in a political setting, being determined by the views and interests of the key players in this setting: politicians, special interest groups, bureaucrats, and academic scholars. This implies that the policy does not generally, if ever, adhere to the principles of economic or public finance theory alone; that more often than not, energy tax policy may compound existing distortions, rather than correct them.[1]

The idea of applying tax policy instruments to the energy markets is not new, but until the 1970s, energy tax policy had been little used, except for the oil and gas industry. Recurrent energy-related problems since the 1970s — oil embargoes, oil price and supply shocks, wide petroleum price variations and price spikes, large geographical price disparities, tight energy supplies, and rising oil import dependence, as well as increased concern for the environment — have caused policymakers to look toward energy taxes and subsidies with greater frequency.

Comprehensive energy policy legislation containing numerous tax incentives, and some tax increases on the oil industry, was signed on August 8, 2005 (P.L. 10958). The law, the Energy Policy Act of 2005, contained about $15 billion in energy tax incentives over 11 years, including numerous tax incentives for the supply of conventional fuels. However, record oil industry profits, due primarily to high crude oil and refined oil product prices, and the 2006 mid-term elections, which gave the control of the Congress to the Democratic Party, has changed the mood of policymakers. Instead of stimulating the traditional fuels industry — oil, gas, and electricity from coal — in addition to incentivizing alternative fuels and energy conservation, the mood now is to take away, or rescind, the 2005 tax incentives and use the money to further stimulate alternative fuels and energy conservation. A minor step in this direction was made, on May 17, 2006, when President Bush signed a $70 billion tax reconciliation bill (P.L. 109-222). This bill included a provision that further increased taxes on major integrated oil companies by extending the depreciation recovery period for geological and geophysical costs from two to five years (thus taking back some of the benefits enacted under the 2005 law). And currently, the major tax writing committees in both Houses are considering further, but more significant, tax increases on the oil and gas industry to fund additional tax cuts for the alternative fuels and energy conservation industries. These bills are being considered as part of the debate over new versions of comprehensive energy policy legislation in the 110th Congress (H.R. 6).

This report discusses the history, current posture, and outlook for federal energy tax policy. It also discusses current energy tax proposals and major energy tax provisions enacted in the 109th Congress. (For a general economic analysis of energy tax policy, see CRS Report RL30406, Energy Tax Policy: An Economic Analysis, by Salvatore Lazzari.)

BACKGROUND

The history of federal energy tax policy can be divided into four eras: the oil and gas period from 1916 to 1970, the energy crisis period of the 1970s, the free-market era of the Reagan Administration, and the post-Reagan era — including the period since 1998, which has witnessed a plethora of energy tax proposals to address recurring energy market problems.

Energy Tax Policy from 1918 to 1970: Promoting Oil and Gas

Historically, federal energy tax policy was focused on increasing domestic oil and gas reserves and production; there were no tax incentives for energy conservation or for alternative fuels. Two oil/gas tax code preferences embodied this policy: (1) expensing of intangible drilling costs (IDCs) and dry hole costs, which was introduced in 1916, and (2) the percentage depletion allowance, first enacted in 1926 (coal was added in 1932).[2]

Expensing of IDCs (such as labor costs, material costs, supplies, and repairs associated with drilling a well) gave oil and gas producers the benefit of fully deducting from the first year's income ("writing off") a significant portion of the total costs of bringing a well into production, costs that would otherwise (i.e., in theory and under standard, accepted tax accounting methods) be capitalized (i.e., written off during the life of the well as income is earned). For dry holes, which comprised on average about 80% of all the wells drilled, the costs were also allowed to be deducted in the year drilled (expensed) and deducted against other types of income, which led to many tax shelters that benefitted primarily high-income taxpayers. Expensing accelerates tax deductions, defers tax liability, and encourages oil and gas prospecting, drilling, and the development of reserves.

The oil and gas percentage depletion allowance permitted oil and gas producers to claim 27.5% of revenue as a deduction for the cost of exhaustion or depletion of the deposit, allowing deductions in excess of capital investment (i.e, in excess of adjusted cost depletion) — the economically neutral method of capital recovery for the extractive industries.

Percentage depletion encourages faster mineral development than cost depletion (the equivalent of depreciation of plants and equipment).

These and other tax subsidies discussed later (e.g., capital gains treatment of the sale of successful properties, the special exemption from the passive loss limitation rules, and special tax credits) reduced marginal effective tax rates in the oil and gas industries, reduced production costs, and increased investments in locating reserves (increased exploration). They also led to more profitable production and some acceleration of oil and gas production (increased rate of extraction), and more rapid depletion of energy resources than would otherwise occur. Such subsidies tend to channel resources into these activities that otherwise would be used for oil and gas activities abroad or for other economic activities in the United States. Relatively low oil prices encouraged petroleum consumption (as opposed to conservation) and inhibited the development of alternatives to fossil fuels, such as unconventional fuels and renewable forms of energy. Oil and gas production increased from 16% of total U.S. energy production in 1920 to 71.1% of total energy production in 1970 (the peak year).

Energy Tax Policy During the 1970s: Conservation and Alternative Fuels

Three developments during the 1970s caused a dramatic shift in the focus of federal energy tax policy. First, the large revenue losses associated with the oil and gas tax preferences became increasingly hard to justify in the face of increasing federal budget deficits — and in view of the longstanding economic arguments against the special tax treatment for oil and gas, as noted in the above paragraph. Second, heightened awareness of environmental pollution and concern for environmental degradation, and the increased importance of distributional issues in policy formulation (i.e., equity and fairness), lost the domestic oil and gas industry much political support. Thus, it became more difficult to justify percentage depletion and other subsidies, largely claimed by wealthy individuals and big vertically integrated oil companies. More importantly, during the 1970s there were two energy crises: the oil embargo of 1973, also known as the first oil shock, and the Iranian Revolution in 1978-1979, which focused policymakers' attention on the problems (alleged "failures") in the energy markets and how these problems reverberated throughout the economy, causing stagflation, shortages, productivity problems, rising import dependence, and other economic and social problems.

These developments caused federal energy tax policy to shift from oil and gas supply toward energy conservation (reduced energy demand) and alternative energy sources.

Three broad actions were taken through the tax code to implement the new energy tax policy during the 1970s. First, the oil industry's two major tax preferences — expensing of IDCs and percentage depletion — were significantly reduced, particularly the percentage depletion allowance, which was eliminated for the major integrated oil companies and reduced for the remaining producers. Other oil and gas tax benefits were also cut back during this period. For example, oil- and gas-fired boilers used in steam generation (e.g., to generate electricity) could no longer qualify for accelerated depreciation as a result of the Energy Tax Act of 1978 (as discussed below).

The second broad policy action was the imposition of several new excise taxes penalizing the use of conventional fossil fuels, particularly oil and gas (and later coal). The Energy Tax

Act of 1978 (ETA, P.L. 95-618) created a federal "gas guzzler" excise tax on the sale of automobiles with relatively low fuel economy ratings. This tax, which is still in effect, currently ranges from $1,000 for an automobile rated between 21.5 and 22.5 miles per gallon (mpg) to $7,700 for an automobile rated at less than 12.5 mpg. Chief among the taxes on oil was the windfall profit tax (WPT) enacted in 1980 (P.L. 96-223). The WPT imposed an excise tax of 15% to 70% on the difference between the market price of oil and a predetermined (adjusted) base price. This tax, which was repealed in 1988, was part of a political compromise that decontrolled oil prices. (Between 1971 and 1980, oil prices were controlled under President Nixon's Economic Stabilization Act of 1970 — the so-called "wage-price freeze.") (For more detail on the windfall profit tax on crude oil that was imposed from 1980 until its repeal in 1988, see CRS Report RL33305, The Crude Oil Windfall Profit Tax of the 1980s: Implications for Current Energy Policy, by Salvatore Lazzari.)

Another, but relatively small, excise tax on petroleum was instituted in 1980: the environmental excise tax on crude oil received at a U.S. refinery. This tax, part of the Comprehensive Environmental Response, Compensation, and Liability Act of 1980 (P.L. 96-510), otherwise known as the "Superfund" program, was designed to charge oil refineries for the cost of releasing any hazardous materials that resulted from the refining of crude oil. The tax rate was set initially at 0.79¢ ($0.0079) per barrel and was subsequently raised to 9.70¢ per barrel. This tax expired at the end of 1995, but legislation has been proposed since then to reinstate it as part of Superfund reauthorization.

The third broad action taken during the 1970s to implement the new and refocused energy tax policy was the introduction of numerous tax incentives or subsidies (e.g., special tax credits, deductions, exclusions) for energy conservation, the development of alternative fuels (renewable and nonconventional fuels), and the commercialization of energy efficiency and alternative fuels technologies. Most of these new tax subsidies were introduced as part of the Energy Tax Act of 1978 and expanded under the WPT, which also introduced additional new energy tax subsidies. The following list describes these:

- Residential and Business Energy Tax Credits. The ETA provided income tax credits for homeowners and businesses that invested in a variety of energy conservation products (e.g., insulation and other energy-conserving components) and for solar and wind energy equipment installed in a principal home or a business. The business energy tax credits were 10% to 15% of the investment in conservation or alternative fuels technologies, such as synthetic fuels, solar, wind, geothermal, and biomass. These tax credits were also expanded as part of the WPT, but they generally expired (except for business use of solar and geothermal technologies) as scheduled either in 1982 or 1985. A 15% investment tax credit for business use of solar and geothermal energy, which was made permanent, is all that remains of these tax credits.
- Tax Subsidies for Alcohol Fuels. The ETA also introduced the excise tax exemption for gasohol, recently at 5.2¢ per gallon out of a gasoline tax of 18.4¢/gal. Subsequent legislation extended the exemption and converted it into an immediate tax credit (currently at 51¢/gallon of ethanol).
- Percentage Depletion for Geothermal. The ETA made geothermal deposits eligible for the percentage depletion allowance, at the rate of 22%. Currently the rate is 15%.

- §29 Tax Credit for Unconventional Fuels. The 1980 WPT included a $3.00 (in 1979 dollars) production tax credit to stimulate the supply of selected unconventional fuels: oil from shale or tar sands, gas produced from geo-pressurized brine, Devonian shale, tight formations, or coalbed methane, gas from biomass, and synthetic fuels from coal. In current dollars this credit, which is still in effect for certain types of fuels, was $6.56 per barrel of liquid fuels and about $1.16 per thousand cubic feet (mcf) of gas in 2004.
- Tax-Exempt Interest on Industrial Development Bonds. The WPT made facilities for producing fuels from solid waste exempt from federal taxation of interest on industrial development bonds (IDBs). This exemption was for the benefit of the development of alcohol fuels produced from biomass, for solid-waste-to-energy facilities, for hydroelectric facilities, and for facilities for producing renewable energy. IDBs, which provide significant benefits to state and local electric utilities (public power), had become a popular source of financing for renewable energy projects.

Some of these incentives — for example, the residential energy tax credits — have since expired, but others remain and still new ones have been introduced, such as the §45 renewable electricity tax credit, which was introduced in 1992 and expanded under the American Jobs Creation Act of 2004 (P.L. 108-357). This approach toward energy tax policy — subsidizing a plethora of different forms of energy (both conventional and renewable) and providing incentives for diverse energy conservation (efficiency) technologies in as many sectors as possible — has been the paradigm followed by policymakers since the 1970s. A significant increase in nontax interventions in the energy markets — laws and regulations, such as the Corporate Average Fuel Economy (CAFÉ) standards to reduce transportation fuel use, and other interventions through the budget and the credit markets — has also been a significant feature of energy policy since the 1970s. This included some of the most extensive energy legislation ever enacted.

Energy Tax Policy in the 1980s: The "Free-Market Approach"

The Reagan Administration opposed using the tax law to promote oil and gas development, energy conservation, or the supply of alternative fuels. The idea was to have a more neutral and less distortionary energy tax policy, which economic theory predicts would make energy markets work more efficiently and generate benefits to the general economy. The Reagan Administration believed that the responsibility for commercializing conservation and alternative energy technologies rested with the private sector and that high oil prices — real oil prices (corrected for inflation) were at historically high levels in 1981 and 1982 — would be ample encouragement for the development of alternative energy resources. High oil prices in themselves create conservation incentives and stimulate oil and gas production.

President Reagan's free-market views were well known prior to his election. During the 1980 presidential campaign, he proposed repealing the WPT, deregulating oil and natural gas prices, and minimizing government intervention in the energy markets. The Reagan Administration's energy tax policy was professed more formally in several energy and tax policy studies, including its 1981 National Energy Policy Plan and the 1983 update to this plan; it culminated in a 1984 Treasury study on general tax reform, which also proposed fundamental reforms of federal energy tax policy. In terms of actual legislation, many of the Reagan Administration's objectives were realized, although as discussed below there were unintended effects.

In 1982, the business energy tax credits on most types of nonrenewable technologies — those enacted under the ETA of 1978 — were allowed to expire as scheduled; other business credits and the residential energy tax credits were allowed to expire at the end of 1985, also as scheduled. Only the tax credits for business solar, geothermal, ocean thermal, and biomass technologies were extended. As mentioned above, today the tax credit for business investment in solar and geothermal technologies, which has since been reduced to 10%, is all that remains of these tax credits. A final accomplishment was the repeal of the WPT, but not until 1988, the end of Reagan's second term. The Reagan Administration's other energy tax policy proposals, however, were not adopted. The tax incentives for oil and gas were not eliminated, although they were pared back as part of the Tax Reform Act (TRA) of 1986.

Although the Reagan Administration's objective was to create a free-market energy policy, significant liberalization of the depreciation system and reduction in marginal tax rates — both the result of the Economic Recovery Tax Act of 1981 (ERTA, P.L. 97-34) — combined with the regular investment tax credit and the business energy investment tax credits, resulted in negative effective tax rates for many investments, including alternative energy investments, such as solar and synthetic fuels. Also, the retention of percentage depletion and expensing of IDCs (even at the reduced rates) rendered oil and gas investments still favored relative to investments in general.

Energy Tax Policy After 1988

After the Reagan Administration, several major energy and non-energy laws were enacted that amended the energy tax laws in several ways, some major.

- Revenue Provisions of the Omnibus Reconciliation Act of 1990. President George H.W. Bush's first major tax law included numerous energy tax incentives: (1) for conservation (and deficit reduction), the law increased the gasoline tax by 5¢/gallon and doubled the gas-guzzler tax; (2) for oil and gas, the law introduced a 10% tax credit for enhanced oil recovery expenditures, liberalized some of the restrictions on the percentage depletion allowance, and reduced the impact of the alternative minimum tax on oil and gas investments; and (3) for alternative fuels, the law expanded the §29 tax credit for unconventional fuels and introduced the tax credit for small producers of ethanol used as a motor fuel.
- Energy Policy Act of 1992 (P.L. 102-486). This broad energy measure introduced the §45 tax credit, at 1.5¢ per kilowatt hour, for electricity generated from wind and "closed-loop" biomass systems. (Poultry litter was added later.) For new facilities, this tax credit expired at the end of 2001 and again in 2003 but has been retroactively extended by recent tax legislation (as discussed below). In addition, the 1992 law (1) added an income tax deduction for the costs, up to $2,000, of clean-fuel powered

vehicles; (2) liberalized the alcohol fuels tax exemption; (3) expanded the §29 production tax credit for nonconventional energy resources; and (4) liberalized the tax breaks for oil and gas.

- Omnibus Budget Reconciliation Act of 1993 (P.L. 103-66). President Clinton proposed a differential Btu tax on fossil fuels (a broadly based general tax primarily on oil, gas, and coal based on the British thermal units of heat output), which was dropped in favor of a broadly applied 4.3¢/gallon increase in the excise taxes on motor fuels, with revenues allocated for deficit reduction rather than the various trust funds.
- Taxpayer Relief Act of 1997 (P.L. 105-34). This law included a variety of excise tax provisions for motor fuels, of which some involved tax reductions on alternative transportation fuels, and some involved increases, such as on kerosene, which on balance further tilted energy tax policy toward alternative fuels.
- Tax Relief and Extension Act. Enacted as Title V of the Ticket to Work and Work Incentives Improvement Act of 1999 (P.L. 106170), it extended and liberalized the 1.5¢/kWh renewable electricity production tax credit, and renewed the suspension of the net income limit on the percentage depletion allowance for marginal oil and gas wells.

As this list suggests, the post-Reagan energy tax policy returned more to the interventionist course established during the 1970s and primarily was directed at energy conservation and alternative fuels, mostly for the purpose of reducing oil import dependence and enhancing energy security. However, there is an environmental twist to energy tax policy during this period, particularly in the Clinton years. Fiscal concerns, which for most of that period created a perennial search for more revenues to reduce budget deficits, have also driven energy tax policy proposals during the post-Reagan era. This is underscored by proposals, which have not been enacted, to impose broad-based energy taxes such as the Btu tax or the carbon tax to mitigate greenhouse gas emissions.

Another interesting feature of the post-Reagan energy tax policy is that while the primary focus continues to be energy conservation and alternative fuels, no energy tax legislation has been enacted during this period that does not also include some, relatively minor, tax relief for the oil and gas industry, either in the form of new tax incentives or liberalization of existing tax breaks (or both).

Energy Tax Incentives in Comprehensive Energy Legislation Since 1998

Several negative energy market developments since about 1998, characterized by some as an "energy crisis," have led to congressional action on comprehensive energy proposals, which included numerous energy tax incentives.

Brief History of Comprehensive Energy Policy Proposals

Although the primary rationale for comprehensive energy legislation has historically been spiking petroleum prices, and to a lesser extent spiking natural gas and electricity prices, the origin of bills introduced in the late 1990s was the very low crude oil prices of that period. Domestic crude oil prices reached a low of just over $10 per barrel in the winter of 1998-1999, among the lowest crude oil prices in history after correcting for inflation. From 1986 to 1999, oil prices averaged about $17 per barrel, fluctuating between $12 and $20 per barrel. These low oil prices hurt oil producers, benefitted oil refiners, and encouraged consumption. They also served as a disincentive to conservation and investment in energy efficiency technologies and discouraged production of alternative fuels and renewable technologies. To address the low oil prices, there were many tax bills in the first session of the 106th Congress (1999) focused on production tax credits for marginal or stripper wells, but they also included carryback provisions for net operating losses, and other fossil fuels supply provisions.

By summer 1999, crude oil prices rose to about $20 per barrel, and peaked at more than $30 per barrel by summer 2000, causing higher gasoline, diesel, and heating oil prices. To address the effects of rising crude oil prices, legislative proposals again focused on production tax credits and other supply incentives. The rationale was not tax relief for a depressed industry but tax incentives to increase output, reduce prices, and provide price relief to consumers.

In addition to higher petroleum prices there were forces — some of which were understood (factors such as environmental regulations and pipeline breaks) and others that are still are not so clearly understood — that caused the prices of refined petroleum products to spike. In response, there were proposals in 2000 to either temporarily reduce or eliminate the federal excise tax on gasoline, diesel, and other special motor fuels. The proposals aimed to help consumers (including truckers) cushion the financial effect of the price spikes. The Midwest gasoline price spike in summer 2000 kept interest in these excise tax moratoria alive and generated interest in proposals for a windfall profit tax on oil companies, which, by then, were earning substantial profits from high prices.

Despite numerous bills to address these issues, no major energy tax bill was enacted in the 106th Congress. However, some minor amendments to energy tax provisions were enacted as part of nonenergy tax bills. This includes Title V of the Ticket to Work and Work Incentives Improvement Act of 1999 (P.L. 106-170). Also, the 106th Congress did enact a package of $500 million in loan guarantees for small independent oil and gas producers (P.L. 106-51).

Energy Tax Action in the 107th Congress

In early 2001, the 107th Congress faced a combination of fluctuating oil prices, an electricity crisis in California, and spiking natural gas prices. The gas prices had increased steadily in 2000 and reached $9 per thousand cubic feet (mcf) at the outset of the 107th Congress. At one point, spot market prices reached about $30 per mcf, the energy equivalent of $175 per barrel of oil. The combination of energy problems had developed into an "energy crisis," which prompted congressional action on a comprehensive energy policy bill — the first since 1992 — that included a significant expansion of energy tax incentives and subsidies and other energy policy measures.

In 2002, the House and Senate approved two distinct versions of an omnibus energy bill, H.R. 4. While there were substantial differences in the nontax provisions of the bill, the energy tax measures also differed significantly. The House bill proposed larger energy tax cuts, with some energy tax increases. It would have reduced energy taxes by about $36.5 billion over 10 years, in contrast to the Senate bill, which cut about $18.3 billion over 10 years, including about $5.1 billion in tax credits over 10 years for two mandates: a renewable energy portfolio standard ($0.3 billion) and a renewable fuel standard ($4.8 billion). The House version emphasized conventional fuels supply, including capital investment incentives to stimulate production and distribution of oil, natural gas, and electricity. This focus assumed that recent energy problems were due mainly to supply and capacity shortages driven by economic growth and low energy prices. In comparison, the Senate bill would have provided a much smaller amount of tax incentives for fossil fuels and nuclear power and somewhat fewer incentives for energy efficiency, but provided more incentives for alternative and renewable fuels. The conference committee on H.R. 4 could not resolve differences, so the bills were dropped on November 13, 2002.

Energy Tax Action in the 108th Congress

On the House side, on April 3, 2003, the Ways and Means Committee (WMC) voted 24-12 for an energy tax incentives bill (H.R. 1531) that was incorporated into H.R. 6 and approved by the House on April 11, 2003, by a vote of 247-175. The House version of H.R. 6 provided about $17.1 billion of energy tax incentives and included $83 million of non-energy tax increases, or offsets. This bill was a substantially scaled-down version of the House energy tax bill, H.R. 2511 (107th Congress), which was incorporated into H.R. 4, the House energy bill of the 107th Congress that never became law. After returning from the August 2003 recess, a House and Senate conference committee negotiated differences among provisions in three energy policy bills: the House and Senate versions of H.R. 6, and a substitute to the Senate Finance Committee (SFC) bill — a modified (or amended) version of S. 1149 substituted for Senate H.R. 6 in conference as S.Amdt. 1424 and S.Amdt. 1431.

On November 14, 2003, House and Senate conferees reconciled the few remaining differences over the two conference versions of H.R. 6, which primarily centered on several energy tax issues — ethanol tax subsidies, the §29 unconventional fuels tax credit, tax incentives for nuclear power, and clean coal. On November 18, 2003, the House approved, by a fairly wide margin (246-180), the conference report containing about $23.5 billion of energy tax incentives. However, the proposed ethanol mandate would further reduce energy tax receipts — the 10year revenue loss was projected to be around $26 billion. On November 24, Senate Republicans put aside attempts to enact H.R. 6. A number of uneasy alliances pieced together to bridge contentious divides over regional issues as varied as electricity, fuel additives (MTBE), and natural gas subsidies, failed to secure the necessary 60 votes to overcome a Democratic filibuster before Congress's adjournment for the holiday season. This represented the third attempt to pass comprehensive energy legislation, a top priority for many Republicans in Congress and for President Bush.

Senator Domenici introduced a smaller energy bill as S. 2095 on February 12, 2004. S. 2095 included a slightly modified version of the amended energy tax bill S. 1149; the tax provisions of S. 2095 were added to the export tax repeal bill S. 1637, on April 5, 2004. The Senate approved S. 1637, with the energy tax measures, on May 11. H.R. 4520, the House version of the export tax repeal legislation, did not contain energy tax measures; they were incorporated into H.R. 6.

Some energy tax incentives were enacted on October 4, 2004, as part of the Working Families Tax Relief Act of 2004 (P.L. 108-311), a $146 billion package of middle class and business tax breaks. This legislation, which was signed into law on October 4, 2004, retroactively extended four energy tax subsidies: the §45 renewable tax credit, suspension of the 100% net income limitation for the oil and gas percentage depletion allowance, the $4,000 tax credit for electric vehicles, and the deduction for clean fuel vehicles (which ranges from $2,000 to $50,000). The §45 tax credit and the suspension of the 100% net income limitation had each expired on January 1, 2004; they were retroactively extended through December 31, 2005. The electric vehicle credit and the clean-vehicle income tax deduction were being phased out gradually beginning on January 1, 2004. P.L. 108-311 arrested the phase-down — providing 100% of the tax breaks — through 2005, but resumed it beginning on January 1, 2006, when only 25% of the tax break was available. (For more information, see CRS Report RL32265, Expired and Expiring Energy Tax Incentives, by Salvatore Lazzari.)

The American Jobs Creation Act of 2004 (P.L. 108-357), commonly referred to as the "FSC-ETI" or "jobs" bill, was enacted on October 22, 2004. It included about $5 billion in energy tax incentives.

ENERGY ACTION IN THE 109TH CONGRESS

The 109th Congress enacted the Energy Policy Act of 2005 (P.L. 109-58), which included the most extensive amendments to U.S. energy tax laws since 1992, and the Tax Relief and Health Care Act of 2006, which extended the energy tax subsidies enacted under the 2005 Energy Policy Act (EPACT05).

The Energy Policy Act of 2005 (P.L. 109-58)

On June 28, 2005, the Senate approved by an 85-12 vote a broadly based energy bill (H.R. 6) with an 11-year, $18.6 billion package of energy tax breaks tilted toward renewable energy resources and conservation. Joint Committee on Taxation figures released on June 28 show that the bill included about $0.2 billion in non-energy tax cuts and more than $4.7 billion in revenue offsets, meaning the bill had a total tax cut of $18.8 billion over 11 years, offset by the $4.7 billion in tax increases. The House energy bill, which included energy tax incentives totaling about $8.1 billion over 11 years, and no tax increases, was approved in April. This bill was weighted almost entirely toward fossil fuels and electricity supply. On July 27, 2005, the conference committee on H.R. 6 reached agreement on $11.1 billion of energy tax incentives, including $3 billion in tax increases (both energy and non-energy). The distribution of the cuts by type of fuel for each of the three versions of H.R. 6 is shown in Table 1.

One way to briefly compare the two measures is to compare revenue losses from the energy tax incentives alone and the percentage distribution by type of incentive as a percent of the net energy tax cuts (i.e., the columns marked "%" divided by the dollar figures in row 11). The net revenue losses over an 11-year time frame from FY2005 to FY2015 were estimated by the Joint Committee on Taxation. The total revenue losses are reported in two ways. The absolute dollar value of tax cuts over 11 years and the percentage distribution of total revenue losses by type of incentive for each measure.

Table 1 shows that the conference report provided about $1.3 billion for energy efficiency and conservation, including a deduction for energy-efficient commercial property, fuel cells, and micro-turbines, and $4.5 billion in renewables incentives, including a two-year extension of the tax code §45 credit, renewable energy bonds, and business credits for solar. A $2.6 billion package of oil and gas incentives included seven-year depreciation for natural gas gathering lines, a refinery expensing provision, and a small refiner definition for refiner depletion. A nearly $3 billion coal package provided for an 84-month amortization for pollution control facilities and treatment of §29 as a general business credit. More than $3 billion in electricity incentives leaned more toward the House version, including provisions providing 15-year depreciation for transmission property, nuclear decommissioning provisions, and a nuclear electricity production tax credit. It also provided for the five-year carryback of net operating losses of certain electric utility companies. A Senate-passed tax credit to encourage the recycling of a variety of items, including paper, glass, plastics, and electronic products, was dropped from the final version of the energy bill (H.R. 6). Instead, conferees included a provision requiring the Treasury and Energy departments to conduct a study on recycling. The House approved the conference report on July 28, 2005; the Senate on June 28, 2005, one month later on July 28, 2005, clearing it for the President's signature on August 8 (P.L. 109-58).

Four revenue offsets were retained in the conference report: reinstatement of the Oil Spill Liability Trust Fund; extension of the Leaking Underground Storage Tank (LUST) trust fund rate, which would be expanded to all fuels; modification of the §197 amortization, and a small increase in the excise taxes on tires. The offsets total roughly $3 billion compared with nearly $5 billion in the Senate-approved H.R. 6. Because the oil spill liability tax and the Leaking Underground Storage Tank financing taxes are imposed on oil refineries, the oil and gas refinery and distribution sector (row 2 of Table 1) received a net tax increase of $1,769 ($2,857-$1,088).

The Tax Increase Prevention and Reconciliation Act (P.L. 109-222)

After expanding energy tax incentives in the EPACT05, the 109th Congress moved to rescind oil and gas incentives, and even to raise energy taxes on oil and gas, in response to the high energy prices and resulting record oil and gas industry profits. Many bills were introduced in the 109th Congress to pare back or repeal the oil and gas industry tax subsidies and other loopholes, both those enacted under EPACT05 as well as those that preexisted EPACT05. Many of the bills focused on the oil and gas exploration and development

(EandD) subsidy — expensing of intangible drilling costs (IDCs). This subsidy, which has been in existence since the early days of the income tax, is available to integrated and independent oil and gas companies, both large and small alike. [3] It is an exploration and development incentive, which allows the immediate tax write-off of what economically are capital costs, that is, the costs of creating a capital asset (the oil and gas well).

Public and congressional outcry over high crude oil and product prices, and the oil and gas industry's record profits, did lead to a paring back of one of EPACT05's tax subsidies: two-year amortization, rather than capitalization, of geological and geophysical (GandG) costs, including those associated with abandoned wells (dry holes). Prior to the EPACT05, GandG costs for dry holes were expensed in the first year and for successful wells they were capitalized, which is consistent with economic theory and accounting principles. The Tax Increase Prevention and Reconciliation Act, (P.L. 109-222), signed into law May 2006, reduced the value of the subsidy by raising the amortization period from two years to five years, still faster than the capitalization treatment before the 2005 act, but slower than the treatment under that act. The higher amortization period applies only to the major integrated oil companies — independent (unintegrated) oil companies may continue to amortize all GandG costs over two years — and it applies to abandoned as well as successful properties. This change increased taxes on major integrated oil companies by an estimated $189 million over 10 years, effectively rescinding about 20% of the nearly $1.1 billion 11-year tax for oil and gas production under EPACT05.

The Tax Relief and Health Care Act of 2006 (P.L. 109-432)

At the end of 2006, the 109th Congress enacted a tax extenders package that included extension of numerous renewable energy and excise tax provisions. Many of the renewable energy provision in this bill had already been extended under the Energy Policy Act of 2005 and were not set to expire until the end of 2007 or later. The Tax Relief and Health Care Act of 2006 provided for one-year extensions of these provisions.

CURRENT POSTURE OF ENERGY TAX POLICY

The above background discussion of energy tax policy may be conveniently summarized in Table 2, which shows current energy tax provisions — both special (or targeted) energy tax subsidies and targeted energy taxes — and related revenue effects. A minus sign ("-") indicates revenue losses, which means that the provision is a tax subsidy or incentive, intended to increase the subsidized activity (energy conservation measures or the supply of some alternative and renewable fuel or technology); no minus sign means that the provision is a tax, which means that it should reduce supply of, or demand for, the taxed activity (either conventional fuel supply, energy demand, or the demand for energy-using technologies, such as cars).

Note that the table defines those special or targeted tax subsidies or incentives as those that are due to provisions in the tax law that apply only to that particular industry and not to others. Thus, for example, in the case of the oil and gas industry, the table excludes tax subsidies and incentives of current law that may apply generally to all businesses but that may also confer tax benefits to it. There are numerous such provisions in the tax code; a complete listing of them is beyond the scope of this report. However, the following example illustrates the point: The current system of depreciation allows the writeoff of equipment and structures somewhat faster than would be the case under both general accounting principles and economic theory; the Joint Committee on Taxation treats the excess of depreciation deductions over the alternative depreciation system as a tax subsidy (or "tax expenditure"). In FY2006, the JCT estimates that the aggregate revenue loss from this accelerated depreciation deduction (including the expensing under IRC §179) is $6.7 billion. A certain, but unknown, fraction of this revenue loss or tax benefits accrues to the domestic oil and gas industry, but separate estimates are unavailable. This point applies to all the industries reflected in Table 2.

ENERGY TAX POLICY IN THE 110TH CONGRESS

Continued high crude oil and petroleum product prices and oil and gas industry profits, and the political realignment of the Congress resulting from the 2006 Congressional elections continued the energy policy shift toward increased taxes on the oil and gas industry, and the emphasis on energy conservation and alternative and renewable fuels rather than conventional hydrocarbons. [4] In the 110th Congress, the shift became reflected in proposals to reduce oil and gas production incentives or subsidies, which were initially incorporated into, but ultimately dropped from comprehensive energy policy legislation. In the debate over these two comprehensive energy bills, raising taxes on the oil and gas industry, by either repealing tax incentives enacted under EPACT05, by introducing new taxes on the industry, or by other means was a key objective, motivated by the feeling that additional tax incentives were unnecessary — record crude oil and gasoline prices and industry profits provides sufficient (if not excessive) incentives.

The (Failed) Compromise Bill

In the House, action in 2007 focused on the Speaker's announced "Energy Independence Day" initiative (H.R. 3221), which combined bills approved by several House committees, including the energy tax provisions approved by the Ways and Means Committee H.R. 2776. [5] H.R. 2776 provided $16 billion in tax incentives, including a four-year extension in renewable energy tax credits under IRC § 45(d) for facilities placed in service after December 31, 2008. It also would have added a tax credit for businesses constructing facilities to produce energy from waves, tides, and other marine sources. The bill would largely have been paid for by rescinding the IRC §199 manufacturing tax deduction for oil and gas producers and by streamlining the tax treatment of foreign oil-related income so it is treated the same as foreign oil and gas extraction income. The House passed H.R. 2776 August 4, by a vote of 221-189. Upon passage, the tax provisions were folded into H.R. 3221.

On the Senate side, the Senate Finance Committee's (SFC) on June 19, 2007, approved a package of tax provisions to be added to the comprehensive energy bill (H.R. 6) by a vote of 15-5. The energy tax bill (the Energy Advancement and Investment Act) proposed a $32.2

billion tax cut for alternative fuels and energy conservation, more than double the size of the W/M bill, to be offset by $32.2 billion of tax increases primarily on the domestic oil and gas industry, but including $4 billion of taxes from disallowing losses on abusive SILO (sale-in, lease out) transactions, and by several other relatively minor tax increases. The proposed tax increases on the domestic oil and gas industry total nearly $27 billion over ten years and account for about 83% of the proposed tax increases. The Senate failed June 21, 2007, to limit debate on the tax title when it was pending as an amendment to the In early December 2007, it appeared that the conferees had reached agreement on a comprehensive energy bill, the Energy Independence and Security Act, and particularly on the controversial energy tax provisions. The compromise on the energy tax title proposed to raise taxes by about $21 billion to fund extensions and liberalization of existing energy tax incentives. The Senate December 13 stripped the controversial tax title from its version of the comprehensive energy bill (H.R. 6) and then succeeded in passing the bill, 86-8, leading to the President's signing of the Energy Independence and Security Act of 2007 (P.L. 110-140), on December 19, 2007. The only tax-related provisions that survived were (1) an extension of the Federal Unemployment Tax Act surtax for one year, raising about $1.5 billion, (2) higher penalties for failure to file partnership returns, increasing revenues by $655 million, and (3) an extension of the amortization period for geological and geophysical expenditures to seven years from five years, raising $103 million in revenues. The latter provision was the only tax increase on the oil and gas industry that survived. Those three provisions would offset the $2.1 billion in lost excise tax revenues going into the federal Highway Trust Fund as a result of the implementation of the revised Corporate Average Fuel Economy standards. The decision to strip the much larger $21 billion tax title stemmed from a White House veto threat and the Senate's inability to get the votes required to end debate on the bill earlier in the day. Senate Majority Leader Harry Reid's (D-Nev.) effort to invoke cloture fell short by one vote, in a 59-40 tally.

The 2008 Economic Stimulus Bill

On February 7 the House and Senate approved a $152 billion bill (H.R. 5140) to stimulate the economy by cutting taxes and increasing spending. The version approved by the SFC on January 30 was a $157 billion economic stimulus package that was similar to the House-passed bill, but which also included $5.6 billion in energy tax incentives, primarily an extension of many of the energy tax provisions for renewable energy and energy efficiency that were dropped from the comprehensive energy bill, the Energy Independence and Security Act of 2007 (P.L. 110-140). Senate Democrats sought this more comprehensive stimulus package that also included an extension of unemployment insurance benefits, and an increase in funding for the low-income home energy assistance program (LIHEAP). However, a cloture vote to limit debate and move this broader bill forward fell one vote short of the 60 votes needed. The Bush administration also voiced its opposition to the Senate's inclusion of the unemployment insurance extension. Thus, the approved H.R. 5140, which President Bush is expected to sign, did not include extension of energy tax provisions that either have expired or will expire in 2008.

Energy Tax Proposals under Congressional Consideration

Frustrated with the lack of action on energy tax subsidies over the past year, on February 27, 2008, House Democrats introduced another bill (H.R. 5351) that contained $18.1 billion in renewable energy and energy efficiency incentives, with many provisions the same as in prior bills, including increased taxes on the major oil and gas companies. H.R. 5351, the Renewable Energy and Energy Conservation Tax Act of 2008, is a package of energy tax incentives aimed at encouraging the production and use of alternative fuels and renewable forms of energy and for energy conservation. It is a slightly smaller version of the energy tax title that was dropped from H.R. 3221 in December 2007, but slightly larger than the $16 billion bill approved by the W/MC in 2007 (H.R. 2776). The tax cuts would be financed largely by repealing the IRC §199 manufacturing tax deduction for major oil and gas producers, and freezing the deduction for all other oil and gas producers at the current rate of 6%. [6] Additional revenue would come from a provision to streamline the tax treatment of foreign oil-related income so it is treated the same as foreign oil and gas extraction income. In response, the administration threatened to also veto this bill, in part because of its increased taxes on the oil and gas industry. House Speaker Pelosi and other Democrats sent Bush a letter February 28, 2008, urging him to reconsider his opposition to the Democratic renewable energy plan, arguing that their energy tax plan would "correct an imbalance in the tax code."

In the Senate, action appeared at one point to be focused on S. 2642; some also speculated that energy tax legislation in the Senate could be part of a $35 billion budget reconciliation effort, which would allow the tax package to pass with only a simple majority of senators, rather than the typical 60 votes needed to avoid filibuster. (Even if the Senate clears the measure, however, President Bush has threatened to veto it.) At this writing, however, Senate action appears to be focused on the Clean Energy Tax Stimulus Act of 2008 (S. 2821), a $6 billion tax bill introduced by Senators Cantwell and Ensign on April 3. On April 10, this bill was added as amendment (S.Amdt. 4419) to H.R. 3221, which in the Senate became the housing/mortgage relief bill. [7] H.R. 3221, as amended, was approved by the Senate on April 10. S. 2821 is one-third the size of H.R. 5361 and has no offsets.

At this writing, Congressional action on energy tax proposals is being taken along three fronts: First, there is the broad and relatively significant expansion and liberalizations of energy tax subsidies for alternative energy and energy efficiency as embodied in H.R. 6049, the House tax extenders bill. This bill, which was approved by the House on May 21, 2008, combines many of the energy tax incentives in prior bills with bills to extend expiring tax provisions, including expired or about to expire energy tax incentives. Second, several relatively small energy tax provisions (both new provisions, and expansions of existing provisions) are in the farm bill, which is currently in conference. These focus mostly on energy from biomass and agricultural products, such as biogas and ethanol.

H.R. 6049. H.R. 6049, The Energy and Tax Extenders Act of 2008, is a $54 billion bill that would extend more than three dozen tax provisions, including nearly a dozen energy tax incentives, at a cost of nearly $17 billion in lost federal tax revenue over 10 years. It also contains $10 billion to cover the expansion of the refundable child tax credit, a new standard for deduction of property taxes, and alternative minimum tax relief and an extension of already expired provisions, such as the research and development tax credit. It does not include tax increases on the oil and gas industry.

The House approved version of H.R. 6049 is a scaled-back version of the bill approved on May 15 by the House Ways and Means Committee. The five provisions removed from the bill were the creation of a cellulosic biofuels tax credit, a reduction in the ethanol credit, a change in the determination of the ethanol credit, a one-year extension of a provision to encourage contributions of property interests made for conservation purposes, and a comprehensive study of biofuels. These energy tax provisions were stripped from the bill because they are included in the farm bill, which is discussed at the end of this report. The energy tax provisions of H.R. 6049, as approved by the House, are

- *Extension and Modification of §45 Renewable Energy Production Tax Credit.* The bill extends the placed-in-service date for wind facilities for one year (through December 31, 2009). The bill would also extend the placed-in-service date for three years (through December 31, 2011) for certain other qualifying facilities: closed-loop biomass; open-loop biomass; geothermal; small irrigation; hydropower; landfill gas; and trash combustion facilities. The bill also includes a new category of qualifying facilities that will benefit from the longer December 31, 2011 placed-in-service date — facilities that generate electricity from marine renewables (e.g., waves and tides). The bill would cap the aggregate amount of tax credits that can be earned for these qualifying facilities placed in service after December 31, 2009, to an amount that has a present value equal to 35% of the facility's cost. The bill clarifies the availability of the production tax credit with respect to certain sales of electricity to regulated public utilities and updates the definition of an open-loop biomass facility, the definition of a trash combustion facility, and the definition of a nonhydroelectric dam. This proposal is estimated to cost $7.046 billion over ten years;
- *Long-Term Extension and Modification of the Business Tax Credit for Solar, Fuel Cell, Geothermal and Microturbine Investments.* The bill extends the 30% investment tax credit for solar energy property and qualified fuel cell property and the 10% investment tax credit for microturbines for six years (through the end of 2014). It also increases the $500 per half kilowatt of capacity cap for qualified fuel cells to $1,500 per half kilowatt of capacity. The bill removes an existing limitation that prevents public utilities from claiming the investment tax credit. The bill would also provide a new 10% investment tax credit for combined heat and power systems. The bill also allows these credits to be used to offset alternative minimum tax (AMT). This proposal is estimated to cost $1.376 billion over 10 years;
- *Long-term Extension and Modification of the Residential Solar Property Credit (IRC§25D).* The bill would extend the credit for residential solar property for six years (through the end of 2014). The bill would also increase the annual credit cap (currently capped at $2,000) to $4,000. The bill would include residential small wind equipment and geothermal heat pumps as property qualifying for this credit. The bill also allows the credit to be used to offset alternative minimum tax (AMT). This proposal is estimated to cost approximately $666 million over ten years;
- *Sales of Electric Transmission Property.* The bill extends the present-law deferral of capital gain on sales of transmission property by vertically integrated electric utilities to FERC-approved independent transmission companies. Rather than recognizing the full amount of gain in the year of sale, this provision allows gain on such sales to be

recognized ratably over an eight-year period. The rule applies to sales before January 1, 2010. This proposal is revenue neutral over 10 years;

- *New Clean Renewable Energy Bonds ("CREBs").* The bill authorizes $2 billion of new clean renewable energy bonds to finance facilities that generate electricity from the following resources: wind; closed-loop biomass; open-loop biomass; geothermal; small irrigation; hydropower; landfill gas; marine renewable; and trash combustion facilities. This $2 billion authorization will be subdivided into thirds: 1/3 will be available for qualifying projects of State/local/tribal governments; 1/3 for qualifying projects of public power providers; and 1/3 for qualifying projects of electric cooperatives. This proposal is estimated to cost $548 million over 10 years;
- *Carbon Mitigation (Capture and Sequestration) Provisions.* The bill would provide $1.5 billion of tax credits for the creation of advanced coal electricity projects and certain coal gasification projects that demonstrate the greatest potential for carbon capture and sequestration (CCS) technology. Of these $1.5 billion of incentives, $1.25 billion would be awarded to advanced coal electricity projects and $250 million would be awarded to certain coal gasification projects. These tax credits would be awarded by Treasury through an application process, with the applicants that demonstrate the greatest carbon capture and sequestration percentage of total CO_2 emissions receiving the highest priority. Applications will not be considered unless applicants can demonstrate that either their advanced coal electricity project would capture and sequester at least 65% of the facility's carbon dioxide emissions or that their coal gasification project would capture and sequester at least 75% of the facility's carbon dioxide emissions. Once these credits are awarded, recipients that fail to meet these minimum levels of carbon capture and sequestration would forfeit these tax credits. This proposal is estimated to cost $1.422 billion over 10 years;
- *Carbon Audit of the Tax Code.* The bill directs the Secretary of the Treasury to request that the National Academy of Sciences undertake a comprehensive review of the tax code to identify the types of specific tax provisions that have the largest effects on carbon and other greenhouse gas emissions and to estimate the magnitude of those effects. This proposal has no revenue effect;
- *Expansion of Allowance for Property to Produce Cellulosic Alcohol.* Under current law, taxpayers are allowed to immediately write off 50% of the cost of facilities that produce cellulosic ethanol if such facilities are placed in service before January 1, 2013. Consistent with other provisions in the bill that seek to be technology neutral, the bill would allow this write off to be available for the production of other cellulosic biofuels in addition to cellulosic ethanol. This proposal is estimated to be revenue neutral over 10 years;
- *Extension of Biodiesel Production Tax Credit, and Extension and Modification of Renewable Diesel Tax Credit.* The bill extends for one year (through December 31, 2009) the $1.00 per gallon production tax credits for biodiesel and the small biodiesel producer credit of 10 cents per gallon. The bill also extends for one year (through December 31, 2009) the $1.00 per gallon production tax credit for diesel fuel created from biomass. The bill eliminates the current-law disparity in credit for biodiesel and agri-biodiesel and eliminates the requirement that renewable diesel fuel must be produced using a thermal depolymerization process. As a result, the credit will be

available for any diesel fuel created from biomass without regard to the process used so long as the fuel is usable as home heating oil, as a fuel in vehicles, or as aviation jet fuel. The bill also clarifies that the $1 per gallon production credit for renewable diesel is limited to diesel fuel that is produced solely from biomass. Diesel fuel that is created by co-processing biomass with other feedstocks (e.g., petroleum) will be eligible for the 50 cent per gallon tax credit for alternative fuels. This proposal is estimated to cost $456 million over 10 years;

- *Plug-in Hybrid/Electric Drive Vehicle Credit.* The bill establishes a new credit for each qualified plug-in electric drive vehicle placed in service during each taxable year by a taxpayer. The base amount of the credit is $3,000. If the qualified vehicle draws propulsion from a battery with at least 5 kilowatt hours of capacity, the credit amount is increased by $200, plus another $200 for each kilowatt hour of battery capacity in excess of 5 kilowatt hours up to 15 kilowatt hours. Taxpayers may claim the full amount of the allowable credit up to the end of the first calendar quarter after the quarter in which the manufacturer records 60,000 sales. The credit is reduced in following calendar quarters. The credit is available against the alternative minimum tax (AMT). This proposal is estimated to cost $1.056 billion over 10 years;
- *Incentives for Idling Reduction Units and Advanced Insulation for Heavy Trucks.* The bill provides an exemption from the heavy vehicle excise tax for the cost of idling reduction units, such as auxiliary power units (APUs), which are designed to eliminate the need for truck engine idling (e.g., to provide heating, air conditioning, or electricity) at vehicle rest stops or other temporary parking locations. The bill would also exempt the installation of advanced insulation, which can reduce the need for energy consumption by transportation vehicles carrying refrigerated cargo. Both of these exemptions are intended to reduce carbon emissions in the transportation sector. This proposal is estimated to cost $96 million over 10 years;
- *Fringe Benefit for Bicycle Commuters.* The bill allows employers to provide employees that commute to work using a bicycle limited fringe benefits to offset the costs of such commuting (e.g., bicycle storage). This proposal is estimated to cost $10 million over 10 years;
- *Extension and Increase of Alternative Refueling Stations Tax Credit.* The bill increases the 30% alternative refueling property credit (capped at $30,000) to 50% (capped at $50,000). The credit provides a tax credit to businesses (e.g., gas stations) that install alternative fuel pumps, such as fuel pumps that dispense E85 fuel. The bill also extends this credit through the end of 2010. This proposal is estimated to cost $156 million over ten years;
- *Qualified Energy Conservation Bonds.* The bill creates a new category of tax credit bonds to finance State and local government programs and initiatives designed to reduce greenhouse gas emissions. There is a national limitation of $3 billion which is allocated to States, municipalities, and tribal governments. This proposal is estimated to cost $1.027 billion over 10 years;
- *Extension and Modification of Credit for Energy-Efficiency Improvements to Existing Homes (IRC§25C).* The bill extends the tax credits for energy-efficient existing homes for one year (through December 31, 2008) and includes energy-efficient biomass fuel stoves as a new class of energy-efficient property eligible for a

consumer tax credit of $300. This proposal is estimated to cost $1.061 billion over 10 years;

- *Extension of Energy-Efficient Commercial Buildings Deduction.* The bill extends the energy-efficient commercial buildings deduction for five years (through December 31, 2013). This proposal is estimated to cost $891 million over 10 years;
- *Modification and Extension of Energy-Efficient Appliance Credit.* The bill would modify the existing energy-efficient appliance credit and extend this credit for three years (through the end of 2010). This proposal is estimated to cost $323 million over 10 years;
- *Accelerated Depreciation for Smart Meters and Smart Grid Systems.* The bill would provide accelerated depreciation for smart electric meters and smart electric grid systems. Under current law, taxpayers are generally able to recover the cost of this property over the course of 20 years. The bill would cut the cost recovery time in half by allowing taxpayers to recover the cost of this property over a 10-year period. This proposal is estimated to cost $921 million over 10 years;
- *Extension and Modification of Qualified Green Building and Sustainable Design Project Bond.* The bill would extend the authority to issue qualified green building and sustainable design project bonds through the end of 2012. Authority to issues these bonds is currently set to expire on September 30, 2009. The bill would also clarify the application of the reserve account rules to multiple bond issuances. This proposal is estimated to cost $45 million over 10 years;
- *Refund of Certain Coal Excise Taxes Unconstitutionally Collected from Exporters.* The Courts have determined that the Export Clause of the U.S. Constitution prevents the imposition of the coal excise tax on exported coal and, therefore, taxes collected on such exported coal are subject to a claim for refund. The bill would create a new procedure under which certain coal producers and exporters may claim a refund of these excise taxes that were imposed on coal exported from the United States. Under this procedure, coal producers or exporters that exported coal during the period beginning on or after October 1, 1990, and ending on or before the date of enactment of the bill, may obtain a refund (plus interest) from the Treasury of excise taxes paid on such exported coal and any interest accrued from the date of overpayment. This proposal is estimated to cost $199 million over 10 years;
- *Solvency for the Black Lung Disability Trust Fund.* The bill would enact the President's proposal to bring the Black Lung Disability Trust Fund out of debt. Under current law, an excise tax is imposed on coal at a rate of $1.10 per ton for coal from underground mines and $0.55 per ton for coal from surface mines (aggregate tax per ton capped at 4.4% of the amount sold by the producer). Receipts from this tax are deposited in the Black Lung Disability Trust Fund, which is used to pay compensation, medical and survivor benefits to eligible miners and their survivors and to cover costs of program administration. The Trust Fund is permitted to borrow from the general fund any amounts necessary to make authorized expenditures if excise tax receipts do not provide sufficient funding. Reduced rates of excise tax apply after the earlier of December 31, 2013, or the date on which the Black Lung Disability Trust Fund has repaid, with interest, all amounts borrowed from the general fund of the Treasury. The President's Budget proposes that the current excise

tax rate should continue to apply beyond 2013 until all amounts borrowed from the general fund of the Treasury have been repaid with interest. After repayment, the reduced excise tax rates of $0.50 per ton for coal from underground mines and $0.25 per ton for coal from surface mines would apply (aggregate tax per ton capped at 2% of the amount sold by the producer). The bill would enact the President's proposal. This proposal is estimated to raise $1.287 billion over 10 years.

S. 2886 and S. 3089. In the Senate, there are essentially two different versions of tax extenders and energy tax provisions. The Senate's main tax extenders bill, S. 2886 (introduced by Senator Baucus), differs from H.R. 6049 in four major ways: (1) it would extend the energy tax incentives for a shorter period; (2) it does not include the expansion and liberalization of energy tax subsidies; (3) S. 2886 would patch the AMT for one year, whereas H.R. 6049 is silent on this issue; and (4) S. 2886 does not contain offsets, whereas H.R. 6049 does — H.R. 6049 amends the tax treatment of deferred compensation paid by managers of offshore hedge funds, and delays the implementation of the worldwide interest allocation rule. However, on June 9 Senator Baucus unveiled a modified version of S. 2886 that would use the same offsets as H.R. 6049. Under the new plan (no bill number yet), the AMT patch would not be paid for, but the entire extenders package, as well as the liberalization of energy tax subsidies, would be.

Finally, on June 6 Senate Republicans introduced their own legislation (S. 3098) that would patch the AMT and extend individual, business, and energy tax provisions but without paying for them i.e., without offsets. This bill could be offered as an amendment during floor debate. The AMT patch would cover tax year 2008, while most of the remaining provisions would be extended for two years through the end of 2009, including the deduction for state and local taxes and the research and development tax credit. The legislation also includes incentives designed to improve energy efficiency and clean energy production, an extension of alternative fuels and marginal production incentives, and tax administration provisions. The legislation has not yet been scored, but the AMT patch has previously been estimated at approximately $62 billion, while the extensions have been estimated to cost near $50 billion.

S. 3044. S. 3044 would roll back $17 billion in existing tax breaks over 10 years for the largest oil companies and impose a 25% windfall profit tax on major oil companies; revenues would be earmarked to expanding renewable energy development. Regarding the tax breaks, S. 3044 targets two tax code provisions that are not strictly speaking targeted subsidies or tax expenditures, but that provide tax advantages — some believe unfair advantages — or reduce tax liabilities for the industry. First, S. 3044 would rescind the ability of major integrated oil companies from claiming the IRC§199 deduction. Enacted in 2004 as an export tax incentive, this provision in IRC §199 allows a deduction, as a business expense, for a specified percentage of the qualified production activity's income subject to a limit of 50% of the wages paid that are allocable to the domestic production during the taxable year. The deduction was 3% of income for 2006, is currently 6%, and is scheduled to increase to 9% when fully phased in by 2010. For the domestic oil and gas industry, the deduction applies to oil and gas or any primary product thereof, provided that such product was "manufactured, produced, or extracted in whole or in significant part in the United States." Note that extraction is considered to be manufacturing for purposes of this deduction, which means that domestic firms in the business of extracting oil and gas from underground reservoirs or deposits qualify for the deduction. This deduction was enacted under the American Jobs

Creation Act of 2004 (P.L. 108-357, also known as the "JOBS" bill). It was originally a substitute for repeal of the export tax benefits under the extra-territorial income tax exclusion, which was ruled to be in violation of trade laws. [8] Secondly, S. 3044 restricts the ability of major oil and gas companies to claim tax credits for taxes and other payments to foreign governments against the U.S. tax on foreign source income. These two provisions are identical to ones in previous bills (such as H.R. 3221) as discussed above.

As to the windfall profits tax, this provision of S. 3044 also follows earlier bills in that it attempts to recoup for the federal taxpayer some of the windfall or "excess" profits — oil and gas industry profits have reached record levels in recent years — earned by the oil and gas industry as a result of unprecedented high petroleum prices. Whereas earlier bills took various approaches in defining a windfall in the case of the petroleum industry, S. 3044 would assess a 25% tax on the difference between profits in any one year and 110% of the average of profits over the 2002-2006 period. Also, any increased investment in renewable energy over the same base period would be credited toward the tax hence reduce the windfall profit tax liability.

In addition to the tax provisions, S. 3044 would prohibit, and provide penalties for, price gouging by the oil and gas industry, tighten regulation of speculators in offshore oil, and suspend filling of the Strategic Petroleum Reserve. Senate Minority Leader Mitch McConnell offered May 1, on behalf of Senate Republicans, an energy-supply bill (S. 2958), the American Energy Production Act, that would authorize drilling in the Arctic National Wildlife Refuge and lift offshore drilling bans.

Likely Effects on Oil and Gas Prices and Oil Import Dependence

S. 3044, and many of the other energy tax bills to significantly expand and liberalize energy conservation tax subsidies, rely on revenue offsets that primarily increased taxes on the domestic oil and gas industry. In the case of these other energy tax bills, opposition was partly grounded on adverse energy price effects, or price increases: it was argued that eliminating tax subsidies for the oil and gas industry would raise industry tax burdens, which would then induce the industry to raise oil and gas prices. In the case of S. 3044, proponents argue just the opposite: that raising taxes on oil and gas by rescinding the §199 deduction, constraining the use of the foreign tax credit, and imposing a windfall profit tax would help to provide price relief. In general, for reasons explained more fully below, none of the oil and gas tax increase provisions proposed in the bills mentioned above are expected to have significant price effects, either on crude oil or natural gas prices, or refined petroleum product prices, such as pump prices. This is particularly true of the §199 deduction, and restrictions to the foreign tax credit, as explained below. The market price of crude oil and natural gas, or even of refined petroleum products, such as gasoline, would not be expected to decrease very much, if at all. In general, also, the income tax increases are not expected to have real output effects in the short run, although they will cause resources to flow to other industries in the long run as long as these other industries are allowed the manufacturing deduction, which is equivalent to a lower marginal tax rate.

Neutrality of the Corporate Income Tax. The two provisions in S. 3044 and other energy tax bills constitute increases in the corporate income tax and would raise a substantial fraction of the revenues from increased taxation of the oil and gas industry. The larger of the two —

the §199 deduction — would rescind an income tax cut enacted nearly three years ago. To understand why repealing this deduction, whether for oil and gas or any other industry, would not likely have price effects, note that the deduction is effectively equivalent to a reduction in the marginal income tax rate. For example, at the marginal corporate tax rate of 35%, which typically applies to large corporations such as oil and gas producers and refiners, the current deduction of 6% is equivalent to a marginal corporate income tax rate of 32.9% (35% x 0.94) rather than 35%.9 The proposed elimination of this deduction is, thus, equivalent to an increase in the marginal tax rate from 32.9% to 35% for those major oil companies to which this would apply. All other large corporations would continue to face a top marginal tax rate of 32.9%, with the exception of non-manufacturing enterprises (services, for example), which do not qualify for the §199 deduction.

From an economic perspective, that is to say, in theory, increasing marginal tax rates on corporate income would be relatively neutral in the short run — it would have no (or few) price effects and other economic effects. The reason for this is that a firm maximizes profit at the point at which market prices are equal to marginal production costs, and neither are affected by an increase in marginal tax rates — the profit maximizing level of output and price are unaffected by the tax. Thus, while eliminating the deduction — that is to say, raising the corporate tax rate — would increase total (or average) business costs and therefore reduce profitability among the major oil and gas producers, as long as marginal production costs are unaffected, there would be no price effects *in the short run*. Note also that while the current corporate income tax is not a pure corporate profits (or cash-flow) tax, a surtax for oil companies would arguably be an administratively simple and economically effective way to capture any oil windfalls in the short run.

In the long run, however, all taxes distort resource allocation, and even a corporate profit tax (either of the pure type or the surtax on the existing rates) would reduce the rate of return and reduce the flow of capital into the industry. In the long run, eliminating the deduction for the domestic oil and gas industry will raise average production costs, adversely affecting the economics of domestic oil and gas projects as compared to domestic non-oil and gas projects. Generally, rates of return to investments in oil and gas would decline, causing a decline in capital flows to this industry, and an increase in capital flowing to other industries, including foreign industries. This would tend to adversely affect domestic production and increase imports: Domestic oil and gas output would be lower, and imports would be higher than they otherwise would be without the tax increase. However, because of the structure of the world oil market, market oil prices are exogenous to U.S. producers (and gas prices tend to follow market oil prices), even these longer term effects are not likely to affect oil and gas prices. Also, the retail price of refined petroleum products, such as gasoline, to consumers is determined by a complex interplay of world supply and demand market variables rather than a domestic corporate tax increase.

Even in the long run, however, it is important to keep the proposed tax increase in perspective. According to the JCT, repealing the §199 deduction for all oil and gas producers would increase revenues, i.e., the industry tax burden, by over $300 million in FY2008, with an average annual increase of $1.1 billion from FY2008FY2017. By virtually any standard of comparison these increases are small. For example, the Energy Information Administration estimates that the industry earned over $123 billion in profits in 2006.10 A proposed tax increase of $300 million is negligible in relation to this profit level. Even the estimated $1.1

billion average annual tax increase represents only 1.4% of the industry's average profit from 2001 to 2006.

Of course business profits are highly variable in the long run, and a reduction in petroleum prices would commensurately reduce industry profits — it could also result in losses — which implies that the relative burden of §199 repeal might grow. But also keep in mind that EPACT05 reduced taxes on the industry by an average of As to the proposed restrictions to the foreign tax credits, this proposal would also be effectively an increase in the corporate income tax on domestic oil and gas producers operating abroad. Again, owing to the structure of the world oil market and how crude prices are determined in this market, there are likely to be few price effects either in the short or long run. However, raising domestic income taxes by restricting the industry's ability to claim credits against the income taxes imposed by foreign countries might negatively affect the competitiveness of the domestic U.S. oil producers operating abroad and competing with foreign firms that would not have such restrictions.

Similarly, the type of windfall profit tax on oil proposed in S. 3044 is also of the income tax type, which, again is not likely to have price or output effects in the short run. This, however, is not likely to be the case with all windfall profit tax proposals: the excise tax type of proposal likewise would not have price effects on petroleum, but it runs the risk of reducing domestic petroleum output and thus increasing import dependence. [11]

Energy Tax Provisions in the Farm Bill (P.L. 110-234)

It should also be mentioned that there are several, relatively small, energy tax provisions in the farm bill (H.R. 2419), which was just recently enacted (P.L. 110234). [12] These provisions, all intended to promote alternative and renewable fuels from agricultural resources, are

- Cellulosic Biofuels Credit. Cellulosic biofuels can be produced from agricultural waste, wood chips, switch grass, and other non-food feedstocks. The bill includes a new, temporary cellulosic biofuels production tax credit for up to $1.01 per gallon, available through December 31, 2012. This provision is estimated to cost $348 million over five years and $403 million over ten years;
- Comprehensive Biofuels Study. The bill directs the Secretary of the Treasury, in consultation with the Secretary of Agriculture, the Secretary of Energy, and the Administrator of the Environmental Protection Agency, to request that the National Academy of Sciences produce an analysis of current scientific findings relating to the future production of biofuels and the domestic effects of an increase in the production of biofuels. This provision is estimated to have no revenue effect;
- Modification of the Incentives Relating to Alcohol Fuels (Volumetric Ethanol Excise Tax Credit). The bill reduces the 51¢ per-gallon incentive for ethanol to 45¢ per gallon for calendar year 2009 and thereafter. If Treasury makes a determination — in consultation with EPA — that 7.5 billion gallons of ethanol (including cellulosic ethanol) were not produced in or imported into the United States in 2008, the reduction in the credit amount will be delayed. If a determination is made that the

threshold was not reached in 2008, the reduction for 2010 also will be delayed if the Secretary determines 7.5 billion gallons were not produced or imported in 2009. In the absence of a determination, the reduction remains in effect. In the event the determination is made subsequent to the start of a calendar year, those persons claiming the reduced amount prior to the Secretary's determination will be entitled to the difference between the correct credit amount for that year and the credit amount claimed, e.g. between 51¢ per gallon and 45¢ per gallon. This provision is estimated to raise $1.203 billion over five years and $1.203 billion over ten years;

- Calculations of Volume of Alcohol for Fuel Credits. The Internal Revenue Code provides a per-gallon credit for the volume of alcohol used as a fuel or in a qualified mixture. For purposes of determining the number of gallons of alcohol with respect to which the credit is allowable, the volume of alcohol includes any denaturant, including gasoline. The denaturant must be added under a formula approved by the Secretary, and the denaturant cannot exceed 5% of the volume of such alcohol (including denaturants). This provision reduces the amount of allowable denaturants to 2% of the volume of the alcohol as regulated by the Alcohol and Tobacco Tax and Trade Bureau. This provision is estimated to raise $124 million over five years and $124 million over ten years;
- Extension of Tariff on Ethanol. The bill extends the tariff on imported ethanol for two years (through December 31, 2010). This provision is effective on the date of enactment. This provision is estimated to raise $70 million over five years and $70 million over ten years;
- Duty Drawback on Imported Ethanol. This provision clarifies the eligibility for a drawback for jet fuel products. A drawback is a rebate on duties, fees, or taxes paid on imported goods when a U.S. business subsequently exports a "commercially interchangeable" good. Current law permits drawback claims for exported jet fuel on the basis of ethanol imports, even though such jet fuel exports are not blended with the ethanol imports. The Conference Report discontinues this practice for ethanol imports beginning on October 1, 2008, allowing for a phase-out of the current practice. Drawback claims for such imports must be filed by October 1, 2010. This provision is estimated to raise $12 million over five years and $17 million over ten years.

For Additional Reading

U.S. Congress, Senate Budget Committee, *Tax Expenditures: Compendium of Background Material on Individual Provision*, Committee Print, December 2006, 109th Cong., 2nd sess.

U.S. Congress, Joint Tax Committee, *"Description of the Tax Provisions in H.R. 2776, The Renewable Energy and Energy Conservation Tax Act of 2007,"* June 19, 2007 (JCX-35-07).

U.S. Congress, Joint Tax Committee, *"Description of the Chairman's Modification to the Provisions of the Energy Advancement and Investment Act of 2007,"* June 19, 2007 (JCX-33-07).

U.S. Congress, Joint Tax Committee, *Description And Technical Explanation of the Conference Agreement of H.R. 6, Title XIII, "Energy Tax Policy Tax Incentives Act of 2005,"* July 27, 2005.

CRS Report RS21935, *The Black Lung Excise Tax on Coal*, by Salvatore Lazzari.

CRS Report RL33302, *Energy Policy Act of 2005: Summary and Analysis of Enacted Provisions*, by Mark Holt and Carol Glover.

CRS Report RL30406, *Energy Tax Policy: An Economic Analysis*, by Salvatore Lazzari.

CRS Report RS22344, *The Gulf Opportunity Zone Act of 2005*, by Erika Lunder.

CRS Report RL33763, *Oil and Gas Tax Subsidies: Current Status and Analysis*, by Salvatore Lazzari.

CRS Report RS22558, *Tax Credits for Hybrid Vehicles*, by Salvatore Lazzari.

CRS Report RS22322, *Taxes and Fiscal Year 2006 Reconciliation: A Brief Summary*, by David L. Brumbaugh.

CRS Report RL33305, *The Crude Oil Windfall Profits Tax of the 1980s: Implications for Current Energy Policy*, by Salvatore Lazzari.

Table 1. Comparison of Energy Tax Provisions the House, Senate, and Enacted Versions of H.R. 6 (P.L. 109-58): 11-Year Estimated Revenue Loss by Type of Incentive (in millions of dollars; percentage of total revenue losses)

	House H.R. 6		Senate H.R. 6		P.L. 109-58	
	$	%	$	%	$	%
INCENTIVES FOR FOSSIL FUELS SUPPLY						
(1) Oil and Gas Production	-1,525	18.9%	-1,416	7.6%	-1,132	7.8%
(2) Oil and Gas Refining and Distribution	-1,663	20.6%	-1,399	7.5%	-1,501	10.4%
(3) Coal	-1,490	18.4%	-3,003	16.2%	-2,948	20.3%
(4) Subtotal	-4,678	57.8%	-5,818	31.3%	-5,581	38.6%
ELECTRICITY RESTRUCTURING PROVISIONS						
(5) Nuclear	-1,313	16.2%	-278	1.5%	-1,571	10.9%
(6) Other	-1,529	18.9%	-475	2.6%	-1,549	10.7%
(7) Subtotal	-2,842	35.1%	-753	4.1%	-3,120	21.6%
INCENTIVES FOR EFFICIENCY, RENEWABLES, AND ALTERNATIVE FUELS						
(8) Energy Efficiency	-570	7.0%	-3,987	21.4%	-1,260	8.7%
(9) Renewable Energy and Alternative Fuels	0	0%	-8,031	43.2%	-4,500	31.1%
(10) Subtotal	-570	7.0%	-12,018	64.6%	-5,760	39.8%
(11) Net Energy Tax Cuts	-8,010	100%	-18,589	100%	-14,461	100.0%
(12) Non Energy Tax Cutsa	0		-213		-92	

	House H.R. 6		Senate H.R. 6		P.L. 109-58	
	$	%	$	%	$	%
(13) Total Energy and Non-Energy Tax Cuts	0		-18,802		-14,553	
(14) Energy Tax Increasesb	0		0		+2,857	
(15) Other Tax Increases			+ 4,705		171	
(16) NET TAX CUTS	-8,010		-14,055		-11,525	

Source: CRS estimates based on Joint Tax Committee reports.

a. The conference report includes a provision to expand RandD for all energy activities. This provision is listed as a nonenergy tax cut to simplify the table.

b. Energy tax increases comprise the oil spill liability tax and the Leaking Underground Storage Tank financing rate, both of which are imposed on oil refineries. If these taxes are subtracted from the tax subsidies (row 2), the oil and gas refinery and distribution sector suffered a net tax increase of $1,356 ($2,857-$1501); if the taxes are subtracted from all of the industry's tax subsidies (rows 1 and 2), the industry experienced a net tax increase of $224 million ($2,857$2,633). Also, the Tax Increase Prevention and Reconciliation Bill of 2006 (P.L. 109-222), enacted on May 17, 2006, increased taxes on the oil industry by about $189 million.

Table 2. Current Energy Tax Incentives and Taxes:Estimated Revenue Effects FY2007 (in millions of dollars)

Category	Provision	Major Limitations	Revenue Effects FY2007
CONVENTIONAL FOSSIL FUELS SUPPLY (bpd = barrels per day; < indicates less than)			
Targeted Tax Subsidies			
% depletion — oil, gas, and coal	15% of sales (higher for marginal wells); 10% for coal	only for independents, up to 1,000 or equiv. bpd	- 1,200
expensing of intangible drilling costs (IDCs) and exploration and development costs — oil/gas and other fuels	IDCs 100% deductible in first year	corporations expense only 70% of IDCs; remaining 30% are amortized over 5 years	- 1,100a
amortization of geological and geophysical costs for oil and gas	costs amortized over 2 years for both dry holes and successful wells	major integrated oil companies must amortize such costs (for both abandoned and successful properties) over 5 years	- 100
expensing of refinery investments	deduction of 50% of the cost of qualified refinery property, in the taxable year in which the refinery is placed in service	must increase the capacity of an existing refinery by 5%; remaining 50% is depreciated; must be placed in service before January 1, 2012	- 26

Table 2. Current Energy Tax Incentives and Taxes:Estimated Revenue Effects FY2007 (in millions of dollars) (Continued)

Category	Provision	Major Limitations	Revenue Effects FY2007
incentives for small refiners to comply with EPA sulfur regulations	$2.10 credit per barrel of low-sulfur diesel, plus expensing of 75% of capital costs	credit limited to 25% of capital costs; expensing phases out for refining capacity of 155,000-205,000 barrels per day.	- < 50
Tax Credits for Enhanced Oil Recovery Costs (EOR)	IRC §43 provides for a 15% income tax credit for the costs of recovering domestic oil by qualified "enhanced-oilrecovery" (EOR) methods, to extract oil that is too viscous to be extracted by conventional primary and secondary waterflooding techniques.	The EOR credit is non refundable, and is allowable provided that the average wellhead price of crude oil (using West Texas Intermediate as the reference), in the year before credit is claimed, is below the statutorily established threshold price of $28 (as adjusted for inflation since 1990), in the year the credit is claimed. With average wellhead oil prices for 2005 (about $65) well above the reference price (about $38) the EOR credit was not available.	- 200
Marginal Production Tax Credit	A $3 tax credit is provided per barrel of oil ($0.50 per thousand cubic feet (mcf)) of gas from marginal wells, and for heavy oil.	The credit phases out as oil prices rise from $15 to $18 per barrel (and as gas prices rise from $1.67 to $2.00/thousand cubic feet), adjusted for inflation. The credit is limited to 25 bpd or equivalent amount of gas and to 1,095 barrels per year or equivalent. Credit may be carried back up to 5 years. At 2005 oil and gas prices, the marginal production tax credit was not available.	0
nuclear decommissioning	liberalizes tax deductible contributions to a fund in advance of actual decommissioning	in general, the IRS sets limits on the annual amounts made to a nuclear decommissioning fund	- 600
electric utilities	allows net-operating losses (NOLs) to be carried back 5 years, as compared with 2 years for all other industries	only 20% of the NOLs in 2003-2005 qualify	- < 50
disposition of electricity transmission property to implement FERC policy	capital gain recognized evenly over 8 years	proceeds must be reinvested in other electricity generating assets	- < 50

Category	Provision	Major Limitations	Revenue Effects FY2007
tax credit for advanced nuclear power facilities	1.8¢/kWh tax credit	limited to 6,000 megawatts of aggregate capacity; each taxpayer's credit also has a per kWh or power limitation and an aggregate limitation	- < 50
credit for clean-coal technologies	20% for integrated gasification combined cycle (IGCC) systems; 15% for other advanced coal technologies	each system has maximum aggregate dollar limits	- 100
Targeted Taxes			
black-lung coal excise taxes and abandoned mineland reclamation (AML) fees	$1.25/ton for underground coal ($0.90 for surface coal)	coal tax not to exceed 4.4% of sales price (2.2% for the AML fee)	900
oil spill liability trust fund excise tax	$0.05/barrel tax on every barrel of crude oil refined	moneys are allocated into a fund for cleaning up oil spills	150
ALTERNATIVE, UNCONVENTIONAL, AND RENEWABLE FUELS			
Targeted Tax Subsidies			
§29, production tax credit	$6.40/bar. of oil or ($1.13/mcf of gas)	biogas, coal synfuels, coalbed methane, etc.	- 4,500
credits for fuel ethanol and biodiesel	$0.51 blender's credit plus $0.10/gal small producer credit	for biomass ethanol only (e.g., from corn)	- 3,000
tax credit for clean-fuel refueling property	$30,000 tax credit for alternative fuel equipment	per location, per taxpayer (replaces a deduction)	- < 50
§45 credit for renewable electricity	1.8¢/kWh. (0.9¢ in some cases; $4.375/ton of refined coal	wind, closed-loop biomass, poultry waste, solar, geothermal, etc.	- 1,100
alternative fuel motor vehicle (AFV) tax credits	$400-$40,000 credit for each fuel cell, hybrid, lean burn and other AFVs	tax credit is function of vehicle weight, fuel economy, and lifetime fuel savings	- 300
exclusion of interest on state and local bonds	interest income exempt from tax	for hydroelectric or biomass facilities used to produce electricity	- 100
credits for biodiesel	$0.50/gal. of recycled biodiesel; $1.00/gal. for virgin biodiesel	sold at retail or used in a trade or business; applies to oils from vegetables or animal fats	- 122
credit for business solar and geothermal technologies	10% investment tax credit for businesses	utilities excluded	- < 100

Table 2. Current Energy Tax Incentives and Taxes:Estimated Revenue Effects FY2007 (in millions of dollars) (Continued)

Category	Provision	Major Limitations	Revenue Effects FY2007
tax credit for renewable energy bonds	credit equals the credit rate times by the bond's face amount	proceeds must be used for renewable electricity projects. national limit of $1.2 billion in bonds	- < 50
ENERGY CONSERVATION			
Targeted Subsidies			
mass transit subsidies	exclusion of $105/month		- 192
manufacturer's credit for energy efficient appliances	max credit is $50 for dishwashers, $175 for refrigerators, and $200 for clothes washers	amount of credit depends on energy efficiency, energy savings, and varies by year; total annual credit is also limited	- 100
deduction for the cost of energy efficient property in commercial buildings	tax deduction of cost of envelope components, heating cooling systems, and lighting	total deductions cannot exceed $1.80/sq.ft.	- < 50
credit for energy efficiency improvements to existing homes	10% tax credit ($500/home) on up to $5,000 of costs; $50$300 credit for other items	max credit on windows is $200	- 300
exclusion for utility conservation subsidies	subsidies not taxable as income	any energy conservation measure	- < 50
	Targeted Taxes		
fuels taxes (FY2006)	18.4¢/gal. on gasoline	4.4¢-24.4¢ for other fuels	35,000
gas-guzzler tax (FY2006)	$1,000-$7,700/ vehicle weighing 6,000 lbs. or less	trucks and SUVs are exempt	201

Source: Joint Tax Committee estimates and Internal Revenue Service data.

Notes: A negative sign indicates a tax subsidy or incentive; no negative sign indicates an energy tax. NA denotes not available.

a. The revenue loss estimate excludes the benefit of expensing costs of dry tracts and dry holes, which includes expensing some things that would otherwise be capitalized. This is a normal feature of the tax code but confers special benefits on an industry where the cost of finding producing wells includes spending money on a lot that turn out dry. This is probably more important than IDCs or percentage depletion.

REFERENCE

[1] The theory underlying these distortions, and the nature of the distortions, is discussed in detail in a companion report: CRS Report RL30406, Energy Tax Policy: An Economic Analysis, by Salvatore Lazzari.

[2] Tax preferences are special tax provisions — such as tax credits, exemptions, exclusions, deductions, deferrals, or favorable tax rates — that reduce tax rates for the preferred economic activity and favored taxpayers. Such preferences, also known as tax expenditures or tax subsidies, generally deviate from a neutral tax system and from generally accepted economic and accounting principles unless they are targeted to the correction of preexisting market distortions.

[3] As is discussed later in the report, many of the other remaining tax subsidies are only available to independent oil and gas producers, which, however, may be very large.

[4] There is an important economic distinction between a subsidy and a tax benefit. As is discussed elsewhere in this report, firms receive a variety of tax benefits that are not necessarily targeted subsidies (or tax expenditures) because they are available generally.

[5] Note: on April 10, 2008 the Senate substituted, and approved, its housing/mortgage relief amendment as H.R. 3221. (See below for more detail).

[6] First enacted in 2004, this provision allows a deduction, as a business expense, for a specified percentage of the qualified production activity's income subject to a limit of 50% of the wages paid that are allocable to the domestic production during the taxable year. The deduction was 3% of income for 2006, is currently 6%, and is scheduled to increase to 9% when fully phased in by 2010. For the domestic oil and gas industry, the deduction applies to oil and gas or any primary product thereof, provided that such product was "manufactured, produced, or extracted in whole or in significant part in the United States." Note that extraction is considered to be manufacturing for purposes of this deduction, which means that domestic firms in the business of extracting oil and gas qualify for the deduction. This deduction was enacted under the American Jobs Creation Act of 2004 (P.L. 108-357, also known as the "JOBS" bill).

[7] S.Amdt. 4419, i.e., S. 2821, was added to S.Amdt. 4387, which was itself a substitute to H.R. 3221. As discussed in the text of this report, in the House, H.R. 3221 was originally the House's comprehensive energy policy act, which incorporated the energy tax provisions of H.R. 2776. In December 2007, H.R. 3221 failed but was replaced by H.R. 6 which was enacted without energy tax provisions as P.L. 110-140. In the House, the housing/mortgage relief bill is H.R. 5720, which was approved by the House Ways and Means committee on April 9, 2008.

[8] CRS Report RL32652, The 2004 Corporate Tax and FSC/ETI Bill: The American Jobs Creation Act of 2004, by David L. Brumbaugh.

[9] Corporations are currently taxed at 15% of the first $50,000 of taxable income, 25% of the taxable income from $50,001 to $75,000, 34% of the taxable income from $75,001 to $10 million, and 35% of taxable income above $10 million.

[10] Energy Information Administration. Oil and Natural Gas Market Supply and Renewable Portfolio Standard Impacts of Selected Provisions of H.R. 3221. December 2007.

[11] For more information see CRS Report RL33305, The Crude Oil Windfall Profits Tax of the 1980s: Implications for Current Energy Policy, by Salvatore Lazzari.

[12] The Conference Report also contains numerous non-tax provisions to promote alternative and renewable fuels from crops. The Conference Report provides $320 million in mandatory funding for loan guarantees for commercial scale biorefineries for advanced biofuels. It also provides $250 million in mandatory funding to provide grants and loan guarantees for renewable energy and energy efficiency systems for farmers, ranchers, and rural small businesses. The Conference Report also provides $35 million in mandatory funding for grants to support repowering of existing biorefineries with biomass energy systems. Included in the energy title is $300 million in mandatory funding for the Bioenergy Program to provide payments to support the production of advanced biofuels, including biodiesel and cellulosic biofuels. The Conference Report continues the Biomass Research and Development program and provides $118 million in mandatory funding. Competitive grants to educate the public about effective biodiesel use and the benefits of biodiesel are continued with funding of $1 million per year.

In: Energy Policy: Issues, Actions and Consequences
Editor: Quentin V. Harris ISBN 978-1-60692-225-5

Chapter 2

ENERGY EFFICIENCY POLICY: BUDGET, ELECTRICITY CONSERVATION, AND FUEL CONSERVATION ISSUES*

Fred Sissine

ABSTRACT

Energy efficiency issues include research and development (R&D) priorities, funding for climate-related efficiency programs, implementation of equipment efficiency standards, regulation of vehicle fuel efficiency, and electricity industry ratemaking for energy efficiency profitability. The Bush Administration has proposed an Advanced Energy Initiative (AEI) to accelerate hydrogen programs. For the Department of Energy's (DOE's) energy efficiency R&D programs, the Administration seeks $484.7 million, with increases for Hydrogen and Hybrid/Electric Propulsion. The request would cut $74.8 million from the Weatherization Program and eliminate controversial funding earmarks. The House-passed version of the FY2007 Energy and Water Appropriations Bill (H.R. 5427) would fund AEI and cut earmarks. The Senate Appropriations Committee has also approved AEI funding and would cut earmarks even further than the House.

Energy efficiency programs have long been justified for the ability to reduce petroleum use and curb environmental impacts such as air pollution. This made it economically and administratively convenient to have them also serve as part of a low cost "no regrets" policy to reduce greenhouse gas (especially CO_2) emissions. In addition to DOE funding, H.R. 5386 would provide about $100 million for the Environmental Protection Agency's energy efficiency program, and the Senate Appropriations Committee's version of H.R. 5522 would provide about $200 million for energy efficiency-related programs in developing countries.

DOE's implementation of equipment efficiency standards has been a subject of some congressional criticism. The Energy Policy Act of 2005 (EPACT, P.L. 109-58) directed DOE to report to Congress on actions taken to address the concern. In response, DOE issued a schedule for rulemakings on 30 products. EPACT also raised the goals for energy efficiency in federal agencies and provided modest tax incentives for efficiency in certain vehicles and buildings.

---

* This is an edited, excerpted and augmented edition of a CRS Report RL33599, dated August 8, 2006 publication.

Automobile fuel efficiency regulation has been one of the most controversial aspects of energy efficiency policy. The Corporate Average Fuel Economy (CAFE) program for new cars and light trucks achieved significant energy savings through 1985 but has remained relatively flat since then. Critics say that recent CAFE increases for light trucks are too small, given concerns about high gasoline prices, air pollution, and CO_2 emissions. Proponents counter that larger CAFE increases would compromise safety and cause hardship for manufacturers.

The *National Action Plan for Energy Efficiency* aims to defer the need for 20,000 megawatts of new electric power plant capacity. Its success will depend mainly on the ability of state regulators to make energy efficiency profitable for electricity companies, by addressing the link between profits and sales.

Most Recent Developments

On June 29, 2006, the Senate Committee on Appropriations reported H.R. 5427, the Energy and Water Appropriations bill for FY2007 (S.Rept. 109-274). This bill includes funding for the DOE Energy Efficiency Program, which is conducted by the Office of EnergyEfficiencyand Renewable Energy (EERE). Compared with House-passed funding for FY2007, the Senate Committee approved an increase of $66. [1] million (5%) for all EERE programs. Table 3 shows other differences, most notably increases for Buildings and Clean Cities programs; and decreases for Weatherization, Fuel Cells, FEMP, Program Management, and Industry programs.

Compared with FY2006 funding, the Committee recommends an increase of $211.7 million (18%) for EERE R&D and deployment programs. This reflects support for the Advanced Energy Initiative, including an increase for the Hydrogen program ($34.2 million). The main cuts include the Weatherization program (-$42.6 million), Industrial programs (-$9.3 million), and Program Management (-$9.9 million).1 Regarding earmarks, both the House ($26.1 million) and Senate ($15.8 million) figures are much lower than the $76.4 million enacted for FY2006. [2]

For the Environmental Protection Agency's Climate Protection (energy efficiency) Programs (H.R. 5386), the Senate Appropriations Committee approved $105.8 million. [3] Also, appropriations bills for the Department of Agriculture (H.R. 5384) and the Department of State (H.R. 5522) fund energy efficiency programs. [4]

The energy efficiency provisions in the Energy Policy Act of 2005 (P.L. 109-58, H.R. 6) and other bills of the 109th Congress are discussed in the "Energy Efficiency in the 109th Congress" and "Legislation" sections below. [5]

Background

Energy Efficiency Concept

Energy efficiency is increased when an energy conversion device, such as a household appliance, automobile engine, or steam turbine, undergoes a technical change that enables it to provide the same service (lighting, heating, motor drive) while using less energy. The energy-saving result of the efficiency improvement is often called "energy conservation." The energy efficiency of buildings can be improved through the use of certain materials (e.g., attic insulation), components (e.g., insulated windows), and design aspects (e.g., solar orientation and shade tree landscaping). Further, the energy efficiency of communities and cities can be improved through architectural design, transportation system design, and land use planning. Thus, energy efficiency involves all aspects of energy production, distribution, and end-use.

These ideas of "efficiency" and "conservation" contrast with "curtailment," which decreases output (e.g., turning down the thermostat) or services (e.g., driving less) to curb energy use. That is, energy curtailment occurs when saving energy causes a reduction in services or sacrifice of comfort. Curtailment is often employed as an emergency measure.

Energy efficiency is often viewed as a resource option like coal, oil, or natural gas. In contrast to supply options, however, the downward pressure on energy prices created by energy efficiency comes from demand reductions instead of increased supply. As a result, energy efficiency can reduce resource use and environmental impacts. An important aspect of energy efficiency policy is to weigh such benefits against the cost of energy efficiency investments.

Energy Efficiency Drivers

Various concerns and national interests drive energy efficiency policymaking. Recently, high energy prices and concerns about energy security have renewed an emphasis on energy efficiency and energy conservation to dampen electricity, natural gas, and oil demand. Energy efficiency is also driven by the potential benefits of avoiding environmental costs that would otherwise result from growth in energy supply facilities, with the attendant impacts of their effluents and emissions on land, water, air, and global climate. Further, energy efficiency is often driven by the potential to reduce consumer energy costs, but this potential can be compromised by several barriers, including perceived threats to the profitability of energy supply companies, the complexity of energy consumer decision-making, and the "rebound effect," wherein expected savings are reduced by increased consumption elsewhere. [6]

Measuring Energy Efficiency and Energy Savings

Measurement Challenge. In the processes of extracting and producing energy, energy supplies are physically tangible and easily measured. In contrast, measuring energy savings and energy efficiency is more challenging. In effect, one is attempting to measure something that never happens; namely, that consumption falls below a projected level and the difference is attributed to the installation of more energy efficient equipment. [7]

Measuring Energy Savings by Individuals and Programs. The scientific approach to measuring the impact of an energy efficiency program is known as evaluation research. [8] This technique employs surveys of actions taken by many of the individuals that receive benefits from an energy efficiency or energy conservation program. Due to the large scale of national programs and the associated cost to mount a large evaluation effort, only a few major evaluations of DOE programs have been conducted, mostly during the 1980s and early 1990s. [9] These studies focused on assessing the energy savings from grant programs. [10]

Evaluating impacts from R&D programs is conceptually, and mechanically, much more difficult than evaluating grant programs. [11]

NAS Study of Barriers to Action by Individuals. More than 20 years ago, the National Academy of Sciences (NAS) prepared a landmark study of the decision-making behavior of energy users. The report reviewed several studies that found energy users often avoid making substantial investments in energy efficiency measures that would have been cost-effective. In particular, NAS observed that some major studies found that only 30% to 80% of economically justified investment would be induced by energy price signals. Further, it found that a belief in market effectiveness persists, despite evidence that institutional barriers to investment in energy efficiency tend to blunt the effect of market signals. The report identifies several technical, market, and information barriers to consumer investment in cost-effective energy efficiency. In particular, NAS focused on the non-rational "folk" model of consumer energy decision-making:

> People who try to make rational calculations based on their own assumptions [folk model] about energy would be led to make fewer energy-saving investments than an expert analyst would recommend ... they [would] interpret their investments as less effective than would an expert.... [12]

In addition, NAS points out that non-technical and non-economic factors have a major impact on energy use:

> More fundamentally, there is a problem with the very notion of users as investors. People do not see their purchases of energy and energy-using equipment only as investment; they have meanings unrelated to the cost of fuel. Car purchasers, for example, do not look solely at fuel efficiency. They are also concerned with performance, safety, styling, status considerations, and other factors. [13]

The report finds similar aspects are factored into decisions about home improvements that have major implications for household energy use.

Measuring the Rebound Effect. One important behavioral aspect of energy efficiency is the "rebound effect." This effect may reduce the measured level of energy (and cost) savings from an energy efficiency action well below the expected level. The rebound can take the form of a direct effect, where resource use is increased (e.g. drive an efficient car more miles); an indirect effect, where additional goods are purchased that use the same resource (e.g. buy a new electrical appliance for the home); or a market effect, where a lower resource price makes new uses affordable (e.g. provide electric heating for a hot tub). Studies have shown that the rebound for automobiles ranges from 10% to 30% and the rebound for home water heating ranges from 10% to 40%. However, in each case, the losses in expected energy savings are generally associated with gains in equipment service (e.g., more hours of use) or increased comfort (e.g., a more desirable temperature setting). [14]

DOE's Efforts To Measure Energy Efficiency in the Economy. In 1989, [15] and again in 1995, DOE prepared a report that attempted to estimate the energy savings from its energy efficiency and energy conservation programs. [16] From 1985 to 2005, national energy use climbed about 20 Q (quads), [17] reaching a record high of 99.9 Q in 2005. DOE's 1995 report Energy Conservation Trends found that energy efficiency and conservation activities from 1973 through 1991 curbed the pre-1973 growth trend in annual primary energy use by about 18 Q, an 18% reduction. In 1992, DOE said this was saving the economy about $150 billion annually in total U.S. energy expenditures.

These two studies used an economic modeling approach to estimate past energy savings trends, distinguish program savings from price-induced savings, and energy savings for each end-use sector. The 1995 report concluded with four basic "lessons" that provide guidance for policy development: (1) energy prices strongly affect trends in energy savings, (2) growth and structural change make energy conservation a moving target subject to continued reevaluation, (3) trends in energy savings reflect a diversity of responses among and within each sector of the economy, and (4) several areas of rising demand are diminishing or detracting from the gains in energy savings, [18] and they present targets of opportunity for further policy attention. [19]

EIA's Approach: Measure Energy Intensity of the Economy. In 1995, EIA issued a report that attempted to address difficulties in measuring energy efficiency. [20] The report declares that the ability to define and measure energy efficiency is essential to the DOE objective of promoting energy efficiency to help the nation manage its energy resources:

> In the absence of defensible energy efficiency measures, any change in consumption might be equated with a change in energy efficiency even if such fluctuations are caused by structural or behavioral effects. [21]

To contribute to the goal of accurately measuring energy efficiency, EIA developed an approach based on energy intensity.

EIA notes that the task of defining and measuring energy efficiency and creating statistical measures as descriptors is a "daunting one." Specifically, it explains that

> [c]hange in energy use over time is driven by a combination of efficiency, weather, behavioral, and structural effects that may be only partially separable and may differ among energy services.... As a practical matter, it is virtually impossible to remove, or even to consider, all of the behavioral or structural factors that would be necessary to obtain a pure measurement of energy efficiency, however broadly energy efficiency may be defined. [22]

Thus, in this view, because energy efficiency is tied to energy use and demand, it must somehow be separated from other factors that affect demand, especially structural (economy), weather, and behavioral effects. [23]

EIA suggested that one way to achieve this separation was to focus on energy intensity as a measurement indicator of energy efficiency. The energy intensity indicator was obtained from an equation in which energy consumption is set equal to the product of energy intensity (energy use rate per unit of service) times the total amount of service provided. [24] EIA says it adopted a comprehensive approach that starts the measurement process with the broadest available measures of energy use and demand indicators. Over time, changes in such measures reflect changes in behavior, weather, structure, and energy efficiency. Further, structures of energy measures are needed that make it possible to separate the effects unrelated to energy efficiency. [25] EIA observes that some of the obstacles to measuring energy efficiency on an economy-wide basis are lack of consistent data, difficulties in establishing demand indicators, and absence of clarity in identifying structural and behavioral influences on efficiency. [26]

EIA's report concluded that further work is needed to forge a consensus on the definition of energy efficiency and the development of energy-intensity indicators that are precise, valid, reproducible, and as robust as possible. EIA offered its report as a focus point for further discussion and debate to improve energy efficiency measures. [27]

EIA's discussion of energy efficiency measurement was continued with an article on its website. [28] The article noted that there are data access and processing barriers to developing energy efficiency indicators. Further, the effort to create international comparative indicators is made more difficult due to structural, behavioral, and economic differences between nations. Even a measure of energy intensity, such as energy use per unit of gross domestic product (GDP), is difficult because of differing measures of energy, currencies, and income accounts.

EIA suggests that different policy contexts call for the use of different energy intensity indicators. For example, a focus on climate change policy might call for an indicator that shows carbon emissions in absolute terms or expressed per unit of energy use. In contrast, a focus on economic productivity policy might call for an indicator that shows energy expenditures per dollar of GDP. EIA said that intensity may only be a "rough surrogate" for energy efficiency, because it may mask structural and behavioral changes that do not represent "true" efficiency improvements. Nevertheless, as with its 1995 report, EIA again found that energy intensity may be the best indicator of energy efficiency that can be developed with available data:

> Energy intensity is defined as the ratio of energy consumption to some measure of demand for energy services. The choice of measure of demand for energy services (a "demand indicator") in efficiency analysis is critical. As examples, in the transportation sector, intensity measures could include gallons per passenger mile or gallons per vehicle mile. Passenger mile and vehicle are the demand indicators in these two examples. [29]

EIA reported that there are four frequently used approaches to developing energy intensity indicators and indexes to measure relative changes, [30] each with its own strengths and weaknesses. [31]

EIA noted that the measurement of energy efficiency and energy intensity can also be affected by the choice between primary energy and site energy as the indicator of energy use. Primary energy is defined as the amount of energy delivered to an end user (e.g., residential housing unit) adjusted to account for losses in generation, transmission, and distribution. [32] Site energy is defined as the amount of energy delivered to an end user without adjusting for these losses. [33] EIA said primary energy is better for constructing aggregate indicators (e.g., energy use/GDP) and for showing ultimate resource or environmental impact; for example, attributing CO_2 emissions to residential electricity use. When the focus is finding differences in end-use efficiency, for example residential air conditioning compared over time, using a simple measure of site energy would be sufficient and may avoid distortions from changes in "upstream"efficiency. EIA asserted that from an economist's viewpoint, using cost expenditures instead of primary or site energy may be preferable. [34]

DOE Program History

From 1974 through 1992, Congress established several complementary programs, primarily at the Department of Energy (DOE), to implement energy saving measures in virtually every sector of societal activity. These energy efficiency and energy conservation programs were created originally in response to national oil import security and economic stability concerns. In the early 1980s, states and utilities took an active role in promoting energy efficiency as a cost-saving "demand-side management" tool for avoiding expensive powerplant construction. Energy efficiency is also viewed as a tool for mitigating environmental problems such as air pollution and global climate change. This aspect spawned new programs at DOE and at several other agencies, including the Environmental Protection Agency (EPA), the Agency for International Development (AID), and the World Bank's Global Environment Facility (GEF). Energy efficiency is increasingly viewed as an important element of sustainable development and economic growth.

The DOE energy efficiency program includes R&D funding, grants to state and local governments, and a regulatory framework of appliance efficiency standards and voluntary guidelines for energy efficient design in buildings. In addition, its budget supports regulatory programs for energy efficiency goals in federal agencies and standards for consumer products. [35]

From FY1978 through FY2005, DOE spent about $12.4 billion in 2005 constant (real) dollars for energy efficiency R&D, which amounts to about 15% of the total

DOE spending for energy R&D during that period. In 2005 constant dollars, energy efficiency R&D funding declined from $692 million in FY1980 to $223 million in FY1988 and then climbed to $652 million in FY2001. For FY2005, a combined total of $467 million was appropriated for the Hydrogen, Fuel Cells, Vehicles, Buildings, and Industrial Technologies Programs. [36] Also, in 2005 constant dollars, from FY1978 through FY2005, DOE spent about $8.2 billion on grants for state and local conservation programs.

This spending history can be viewed within the context of DOE spending for the three major energy supply R&D programs: nuclear, fossil, and renewable energy R&D. From FY1948 through FY1977, in 2005 constant dollars, the federal government spent about $42.6 billion for nuclear (fission and fusion) R&D and about $14.1 billion for fossil energy R&D. [37] From FY1978 through FY2005, the federal government spent $33.9 billion for nuclear (fission and fusion), $21.1 billion for fossil, $13.4 billion for renewables, and $12.4 billion for energy efficiency. [38] Thus, total energy R&D spending from FY1948 to FY2005, in 2005 constant dollars, reached $140.0 billion, including $76.3 billion, or 55%, for nuclear; $35.2 billion, or 25%, for fossil; $13.4 billion, or 10%, for renewables; and $12.4 billion, or 9%, for energy efficiency.

Under the FY2005 budget structure (in current 2005 dollars) for EERE, DOE's energy efficiency R&D funding totaled $595.9 million, or about 25% of DOE's energy R&D appropriation. Renewable energyR&D received $380.3 million (16%), fossil energy received $539.6 million (22%), and fission and fusion were appropriated $784.1 million (32%).

DOE's Strategic and Performance Goals

In 2004, a National Academy of Public Administration (NAPA) study [39] found dramatic improvement in the Office of Energy Efficiency and Renewable Energy (EERE) after a major reorganization that included two new offices: FreedomCAR and Vehicle Technologies, and Hydrogen, Fuel Cells, and Infrastructure. DOE completed a major office reorganization in 2005. [40]

A 2001 report by the National Research Council (NRC) found that the net economic benefits associated with DOE energy efficiency programs were more than four times larger than the investment in RD&D over a 22-year period. [41] Further, the report found that DOE did not use a consistent method for evaluating project benefits, and recommended that DOE adopt NRC's framework to assess R&D costs and benefits and to prepare reports to Congress required by the Government Performance and Results Act (GPRA). [42] Areas found short of expected benefits were found to have lacked incentives needed for private sector adoption. [43] Further, DOE noted that from 2001 through 2004, EERE was awarded 33 "R&D 100" awards. [44]

A 2004 Resources for the Future (RFF) report, The Effectiveness and Cost of Energy Efficiency Programs, reviews a broad range of studies about DOE and EPA programs. The report estimates that a selected range of non-transportation programs saves four Q of energy per year and estimates carbon and air pollution emission savings. [45]

The President's Management Agenda set out the Bush Administration's framework for performance management based on human capital, competitive sourcing, financial performance, electronic government, and integration of budget with performance. The Government Performance and Results Act (GPRA, P.L. 10362) requires each federal agency to produce and update a strategic plan linked to annual performance plans.

In the DOE Budget Request for FY2007, energy efficiency is addressed under the strategic goal "to protect national and economic security" and within General Goal 4, which seeks to "[i]mprove energy security" through a variety of energy supply measures and by "improving energy efficiency." In support of DOE General Goals, the request lists 10 Program Goals (PGs) under Energy Conservation, from which selected PGs follow. PG 4.01 says the Hydrogen/Fuel Cell Technologies Program will achieve certain cost and performance goals. PG 4.02 aims to increase the efficiency of cars and trucks to "reduce petroleum use and greenhouse gas emissions." PG 4.04 says that the Buildings Program will allow buildings to become "capable of generating as much energy as they consume." PG 4.06 says that the Industrial Technologies Program aims to save feedstock and process energy, improve environmental performance, and improve economic competitiveness. PG 4.13 says that the Federal Energy Management Program (FEMP) will support federal agency efforts to achieve life cycle energy savings of 17 trillion Btus each year from FY2007 through FY2011. [46] DOE estimates that the EERE programs will curb energy demand growth by 8 Q per year in 2025 and by 30 Q in 2050, [47] a savings approximately double that which would otherwise be expected by 2050. [48]

ENERGY EFFICIENCY IN THE 109TH CONGRESS

Action in the Second Session

DOE Budget, FY2007. President Bush issued the Administration's FY2007 budget request on February 6, 2006. The Department of Energy (DOE) request seeks $484.7 million for energy efficiency R&D, which is $20.9 million, or 4.5%, more than the FY2006 appropriation (excluding inflation). The request calls for increased funding for the Advanced Energy Initiative and elimination (or reprogramming) of congressional earmarks.

In his State of the Union address, President Bush announced the launch of the American Competitiveness Initiative (ACI) to stimulate long-term economic growth, in large part by increased promotion of R&D and technological innovation. [49] A key component of the ACI is the Advanced Energy Initiative, [50] which DOE says also "aims to reduce America's dependence on imported energy sources." [51] The Hydrogen Fuel Initiative is one theme under the Advanced Energy Initiative that is funded under energy efficiency programs in DOE's Office of Energy Efficiency and Renewable Energy (EERE). The goal of the Hydrogen Fuel Initiative is to "bring hydrogen and fuel cell technology from the laboratory to the showroom." Specifically, the program aims to "facilitate a decision by industry to commercialize a hydrogen infrastructure and fuel cell vehicles by 2015." [52] To support this initiative, the DOE FY2007 request for energy efficiency programs proposes major funding increases for hydrogen and fuel cell technology programs. Also, the ACI and the FY2007 federal budget reflect strong concern about the "rapidly growing" amount of legislative earmarks for R&D programs, [53] including the Hydrogen program. [54]

The House Appropriations Committee report on the FY2007 Energy and Water Development Appropriations Bill includes several policy directives to EERE. [55] First, the report directs EERE to report by January 31, 2007, on the progress of implementing the Inspector General's recommendations (IG audit report DOE/IG0689) to improve the management of cooperative agreements. [56] Second, it directs EERE to strengthen recruiting from Historically Black Colleges and Universities. [57] Also, one DOE-wide directive that would directly affect EERE involves funding for the Asia Pacific Partnership (APP), which would support clean, energy-efficient technologies. The report directs DOE to submit a reprogramming request if it intends to support APP with FY2006 funds and to submit a detailed budget justification (which would be considered by the conference committee) if it proposes to use FY2007 funds. [58]

The Senate Appropriations Committee report includes several policy directives to EERE, of which two apply to energy efficiency programs. [59] First, it directs DOE to study possible impacts of plug-in hybrid-vehicles on electricity supply and distribution networks, including urban areas, and to study environmental aspects of fuel-switching. [60] Second, it directs DOE to provide a strategy to accelerate the development of zero energy buildings by five to seven years. [61]

Table 1. EPA Funding for Climate Protection Energy Efficiency Programs (CPP) ($ millions current)

	FY2004 Enacted	FY2005 Enacted	FY2006 Appn.	FY2007 Request	FY2007 House	FY2007 Senate	Senate-House
Environ. Programs & Management	88.5	92.5	90.8	91.8	92.6	93.2	0.6
Science & Technology	21.8	20.4	18.6	12.6	18.6	12.6	-6.0
Total	110.3	112.9	109.4	104.3	111.2	105.8	-5.4

Sources: S.Rept. 109-275; H.Rept. 109-465; EPA FY2007 Annual Performance Plan and Congressional Justification, February 2006, [http://www.epa.gov/ocfopage/budget/2007/2007cj.htm].

EPA Budget, FY2007. The FY2007 request for EPA's Climate Protection Programs (CPP), which focus mainly on voluntary energy efficiency activities, is $104.3 million, which is $5.1 million less than the FY2006 appropriation. This includes $1.0 million more under the Office of Environmental Programs and Management (EPM) and $6.1 million less under the Office of Science and Technology (S&T) for transportation activities. [62] The House approved $111.2 million, and the Senate Appropriations Committee approved $105.8 million.

EPA conducts its CPP programs under the Office of Atmospheric Programs, with funding from appropriations accounts for EPM and S&T. EPM programs cover the areas of buildings (Energy Star), industry, state and local government, international, and sequestration. S&T programs cover mainly transportation. These programs include Energy Star Buildings, Methane to Markets, Climate Wise, and Transportation Partners. They involve public-private partnerships that promote energy efficient lighting, buildings, and office equipment. Efforts also include labeling, information dissemination, and other activities to overcome market barriers.

Energy Policy Act of 2005 (EPACT, P.L. 109-58)

Efficiency Standards for Consumer and Commercial Products. DOE currently sets minimum energy efficiency standards for several consumer and commercial products, including household appliances such as clothes washers and refrigerators. P.L. 109-58 (§135 and §136) sets a variety of energy efficiency standards for consumer appliances and commercial equipment. As Table 2 shows, most of the standards are set by law, but some are at the discretion of a DOE rulemaking. The American Council for an Energy-Efficient Economy (ACEEE) estimates that these new standards will save more energy than any other efficiency provisions in the act.

During deliberations over H.R. 6, concern had been raised about delays in the implementation of previously enacted laws that had directed DOE to establish energy efficiency standards for certain equipment. As a result, the final law contains a section (§141) requiring DOE to report regularly to Congress when efficiency standard rulemakings are behind schedule, and to include steps being taken to get back on schedule. [63]

Table 2. EPACT Energy Efficiency Standards

Standard set:	P.L. 109-58 (H.R. 6, Conference)
By law (16 products)	exit signs, traffic signals, building transformers, torchiere lighting fixtures, compact fluorescent lamps, commercial unit heaters, residential dehumidifiers, commercial refrigerators and freezers, large commercial air conditioners, commercial ice makers, commercial clothes washers, pedestrian crossing signals, mercury vapor lamp ballasts, fluorescent lamp ballasts, pre-rinse spray valves (used in restaurants), and residential ceiling fan light kits.
By rule (3 products)	external power supplies, battery chargers, refrigerated beverage vending machines.

On January 31, 2006, DOE released a report to Congress with a schedule for setting new appliance efficiency standards. [64] The report identifies 19 products (in the categories of heating, transformers and motors, lighting, home appliances, and space cooling) for which DOE has missed the deadlines established prior to EPACT. [65] In addition, the report lists 11 products (in the categories of lighting, home appliances, commercial refrigeration, battery chargers, and external power supplies) for which standards are required by EPACT. Since the report, DOE has issued standards for commercial refrigerator and refrigerator freezers (April 25) and for small industrial electric motors (July 10).

Efficiency Goals for Federal Buildings. The purpose of federal efficiency goals is to lead by example in saving energy, reducing costs, and helping transform markets for new equipment. The past goal had called for a 20% reduction in federal buildings' energy use, measured in energy use per square foot (sf), from 1985 to 2000. This goal was exceeded, slightly. P.L. 109-58 (§102) sets a goal for further energy efficiency in federal facilities. Compared with the baseline year energy use in 2003, the goal is a 20% energy reduction over a 10-year period from 2006 to 2015. Also, DOE is required to review results by the end of the 10-year period and recommend further goals for an additional decade. Most of the other provisions for federal programs are administrative measures that would help agencies achieve the above-described goal.

The historical record shows that congressional buildings have had less focus on energy efficiency goals than those in the executive branch. [66] To address this, P.L. 109-58 (§101) calls for the implementation of a plan for congressional buildings to meet the energy efficiency goal for federal agencies noted above. It also calls for a study of the potential for energy efficiency and renewables to increase reliability during a power outage.

Tax Incentives for Efficiency and Conservation. Since the late 1970s, some tax incentives have been enacted to promote fuel switching and alternative fuels as a way to conserve gasoline and reduce oil import dependence. In contrast, tax incentives for energy efficiency and for electricity conservation have been rare and generally short-lived. P.L. 109-58 includes new tax credits for energy efficiency that apply to commercial property, new home construction, existing home improvements, appliances, residential fuel cells, and business fuel cells.

Energy Efficiency Tax Revenue Effect. Table 3, below, compares the estimated 11-year revenue effect of energy efficiency and conservation tax provisions in the House, Senate, and Conference versions of H.R. 6.

Table 3. H.R. 6, Tax Revenue Effect ($ billions)

	House	Senate	Conference (P.L. 109-58)
Energy Efficiency and Conservation Measures (§1312 and §1317 in House bill, excluding diesel fuels, alternative fuels, and solar credit)	$0.397	$3.733	$1.260
Hybrid and Fuel Cell Vehicles	—	$1.686	—
Total, Energy Efficiency and Conservation	$0.397	$5.419	$1.260
Gross Total, All Tax Cut Provisions	$8.090	$18.421	$14.553
Energy Efficiency and Conservation Share of Total	4.9%	29.4%	8.7%

Sources: Joint Committee on Taxation (JCT), Estimated Budget Effects of the Conference Agreement for Title XIII of H.R. 6, July 27, 2005 (JCX-59-05); Estimated Revenue Effects of the Chairman's Amendment in the Nature of a Substitute to H.R. 1541, Scheduled for Markup by the Committee on Ways and Means, April 13, 2005 (JCX-17-05); Estimated Revenue Effects of the Chairman's Amendment in the Nature of a Substitute to the "Energy Policy Tax Incentives Act of 2005," Scheduled for Markup by the Committee on Finance, June 16, 2005 (JCX-47-05).

Housing, Funding Authorizations, and Other Provisions. P.L. 109-58 has several provisions (§151-§154) for energy efficiency in public housing. Also, Section 121 authorizes funding for energy assistance (e.g., Low-Income Home Energy Assistance Program, LIHEAP), and Sections 122 and 123 authorize grant programs (e.g., DOE Weatherization Program and State Energy Program). Several other energy efficiency programs are authorized in Title I and Title IX.

Efficiency's Role in Energy Security, By Fuel

By curbing the demand for petroleum fuels, energy efficiency measures may contribute to energy security by reducing oil import dependence and the risk of oil shortages, energy price shocks, and their attendant impacts on the national economy. By cutting demand for natural gas, energy efficiency may dampen natural gas prices and reduce the need for liquified natural gas (LNG) imports. Also, by curbing the demand for electricity, energy efficiency may reduce the risk of brownouts, blackouts, and other reliability problems.

Electricity Demand-Side Management (DSM) To Improve Reliability

In the early 1990s, many states and electric utilities created demand-side management (DSM) programs to promote energy efficiency and other activities as a less costly alternative to new supply. DSM became a significant part of the nation's energy efficiency effort. Utility DSM spending peaked in 1994 at $2.7 billion, and DSM energy savings peaked in 1996 at 62 billion kilowatt-hours (equivalent to the output from 12 one-gigawatt powerplants). [67] After

California issued its 1994 proposal for electric industry restructuring, many states and utilities reduced DSM efforts. By 1998, utility DSM spending had fallen by nearly half, to about $1.4 billion, and estimated annual energy savings fell to a low of 49 billion kwh. [68] Savings from energy efficiency in the electricity sector climbed slowly thereafter, reaching 55 billion kwh in 2004. [69]

Electricity problems in California in 2001 raised the issue of whether a federal role is needed to encourage demand-side energy efficiency and load management measures. A 2002 report for DOE by the Lawrence Berkeley National Laboratory found that conservation and efficiencymeasures reduced summer 2001 peak demand in California by 10%, increased system reliability, avoided some wholesale power purchases, and avoided $2 billion to $20 billion in potential losses from rolling blackouts. [70]

The August 2003 electric power blackout that affected several states and Canadian provinces rekindled interest in energy efficiency, demand response (demand-side management), and distributed power. The use of energy efficient appliances and other end-use equipment can reduce electricity demand, which drives the need for new power plants.

In late July 2006, a group of more than 50 organizations including the Edison Electric Institute, more than 20 electric and gas utilities, the president of the National Association of Regulatory Commissioners (NARUC), and 16 state regulatory agencies issued a National Action Plan for Energy Efficiency, calling on the electric power industry to pursue a major effort to improve energy efficiency. [71] The Plan was developed with assistance from DOE (Office of Electricity) and EPA (Office of Air and Radiation, Climate Protection Partnerships Division) and is supported by the American Council for an Energy-Efficient Economy, the Alliance to Save Energy, and the American Council on Renewable Energy. The report projects that implementation of the Plan could defer the need for 40 new 500-megawatt power plants, avoid a substantial amount of greenhouse gases, lower the costs of air pollution controls, and reduce prices for natural gas.

The Plan aims to help states and utilities address policy, regulatory, and other barriers that limit energy efficiency investment in more efficient homes, buildings, and industries that would provide energy savings that would cost less than new energy supplies and would reduce energy bills. The five recommendations are (1) recognize energy efficiency as a high-priority energy resource; (2) make a strong, long-term commitment to implementing cost-effective energy efficiency measures; (3) educate the public and policymakers on the benefits of and opportunities for energy efficiency; (4) promote sufficient, timely, and stable program funding to deliver energy efficiency where cost-effective; and (5) modify policies to align utility incentives with the delivery of cost-effective energy efficiency and modify ratemaking practices to promote energy efficiency investments.

The fifth recommendation may be the most important one. It marks a return to the "energy efficiency profitability" issue of the early 1990s, when it was recognized that energy efficiency faced a major economic barrier because, without establishing appropriately compensating policy changes, the reduction in demand would hurt electric industry sales and profitability. One objective of the Plan is to encourage state regulators to modify ratemaking practices so that energy efficiency is cost-effective to a company's bottom line.

Natural Gas Conservation Through Energy Efficiency in Buildings and Equipment

In 2003, the Secretary of Energy requested that the National Petroleum Council (NPC) report on policy options to address the problem of high natural gas prices. The report, Balancing Natural Gas Policy, [72] says gas prices could average from $5 to $7 per thousand cubic feet for years to come, and it concludes, among other options, that energy conservation and greater energy efficiency have the biggest immediate potential to hold down prices. The report recommends updating building codes and equipment standards, promoting Energy Star equipment, using the most efficient power plants, deploying distributed energy, installing smart controls, and employing best practices for low-income weatherization.

The Alliance to Save Energy and the American Council for an Energy-Efficient Economy (ACEEE) applauded the NPC recommendations but stressed that many other measures — including tax incentives, utility performance standards, federal buildings improvements, and regulations to make energy conservation profitable for utilities — were not in the report and should be considered. Further, the 2005 report by ACEEE, Impacts of Energy Efficiency and Renewable Energy on Natural Gas Markets: Updated and Expanded Analysis, says that in a single year, a massive energy efficiency effort could be put in place that would reduce gas use by 1% and cut prices by 37%. [73]

In January 2005, the Senate Energy and Natural Resources Committee held a natural gas conference. Some participants described the potential for energy efficiency to reduce gas demand and prices. [74] Further, some statements refer to a DOE study, Easing the Natural Gas Crisis: Reducing Natural Gas Prices through Increased Deployment of Renewable Energy and Energy Efficiency. [75]

Petroleum Conservation through Energy Efficiency In Vehicles

Energy efficiency measures to curb oil demand, and other oil conservation measures, may help address energy security, economic issues such as high gasoline prices and oil import dependence, and environmental issues such as air pollution and climate change.

The regulation of automobile fuel efficiency to curb petroleum use has been one of the most controversial aspects of energy efficiency policy. The Corporate Average Fuel Economy (CAFE) program for new cars and light trucks achieved significant energy savings through 1985 but has remained relatively flat since then. Critics say that recent CAFE increases for light trucks are too small, given concerns about high gasoline prices, air pollution, and CO_2 emissions. Proponents contend that larger CAFE increases would compromise safety and cause hardship for manufacturers.

Specifically, CAFE required a gradual ramp-up of fuel efficiency for newly manufactured cars and light trucks from 1978 through 1985. [76] The CAFE standard for new cars has remained at 27.5 mpg from model year (MY) 1986 through MY2007. In 2003, the Department of Transportation's National Highway Traffic Safety Administration (NHTSA) issued new light truck (two-wheel drive) standards, setting a standard of 21.0 mpg for MY 2005, 21.6 mpg for MY 2006, and 22.2 mpg for MY 2007. In March 2006, NHTSA raised the light truck standard further to 22.5 mpg for MY 2008, 23.1 mpg for MY 2009, and 23.5 mpg for MY 2010. [77] NHTSA estimates that the new standard will save 700,000 barrels of fuel per day by 2010. [78]

The rollover of new, more efficient cars into the national fleet has gradually raised the overall fleet fuel economy. EIA says the national fleet fuel economy for cars peaked at 21.1 mpg in 1991, declined slightly, and then climbed to 22.4 mpg in 2004. Light trucks have experienced greater variability, with a recent peak in 2001 at 17.6 and a decline to 16.2 mpg in 2004. [79]

The Energy Policy Act of 2005 (P.L. 109-58, §774) requires EPA to revise its adjustment factors to increase the accuracy of automobile fuel economy labels. In deliberations over H.R. 6 (P.L. 109-58), the Senate version of the bill included a provision to save 1 million barrels of oil per day by 2010, but the provision did not survive conference.

A 2003 report by the Congressional Budget Office (CBO), The Economic Costs of Fuel Economy Standards Versus a Gasoline Tax, [80] found that a 46-cent-per-gallon gasoline tax increase would achieve a 10% reduction in fuel use at a cost that is 3% less than the cost of creating a higher CAFE standard, with or without credit trading.

Oil use in transportation can also be reduced through short-term conservation measures such as increased use of public transit, carpooling and ridesharing, and telecommuting; and through curtailment (e.g., driving less) and substitution of alternative fuels. Other measures can help reduce non-transportation oil uses. For example, home improvement measures such as insulation, energy-efficient windows, and weatherization measures can reduce the use of home heating oil.

Energy Efficiency Programs Targeted at Climate Change

Energy efficiency is seen as a key means to reduce fossil fuel-induced carbon dioxide (CO_2) emissions that may contribute to global climate change. Federal efforts to curb emissions through increased energy efficiency may be affected by debates over program appropriations, by the extent to which EPACT's energy efficiency tax incentives are used, and by the rate at which DOE implements EPACT's equipment efficiency standards.

Energy Efficiency and Carbon Dioxide Emissions Projections

DOE's 2000 report Scenarios for a Clean Energy Future projected the potential for advanced energy efficiency and other measures to cut the projected U.S. carbon emissions growth to the 1990 level by 2020. [81] The report assumed a 1990 baseline of 1,346 million metric tons of carbon (MMTC), growing to 1,922 MMTC in a 2020 "business-as-usual" (BAU) estimate of emissions, based on the reference case in EIA's Annual Energy Outlook 1999. [82] Assuming a 50% increase in federal R&D spending on energy efficiency and clean energy, and several sector-specific policy changes, the report develops a Moderate Scenario where 2020 emissions would be constrained to about 1,735 MMTC. Further, the report develops an Advanced Scenario where federal R&D spending doubles for energy efficiency and clean energy, carbon trading is instituted with a permit price at $50 per ton, and several sector-specific policies are enacted, yielding a 2020 emissions level approximately equal to that for 1990. In addition, both scenarios showed net energy cost savings, air pollution reductions, improved balance of payments, and reduced vulnerability to oil supply disruptions. However, the report also found significant adverse impacts on the coal industry, and estimated a reduction in Gross Domestic Product (GDP) that ranged from $4 billion to $66 billion by 2010.

Assuming no major future policy actions, the reference case scenario in the EIA's Annual Energy Outlook 2006 projects 2020 emissions will be 1,942 MMTC, 42% more than that for 1990. [83]

International Context and the "No Regrets" Policy

United Nations. With ratification of the U.N. Framework Convention on Climate Change (FCCC) in 1992, [84] U.S. policy toward global climate change evolved from a "study only" to a more "study and action" orientation. [85] During the FCCC deliberations, the National Academy of Sciences (NAS) released a report stating that "[t]he United States could reduce or offset its greenhouse gas emissions by between 10 and 40 percent of 1990 levels at low cost, or at some net savings, if proper policies are implemented." [86] The NAS's energy policy recommendations included a focus on increasing energy conservation and efficiency. [87]

The Energy Policy Act of 1992 (EPACT92, P.L. 102-486) has been the principal statutory basis for programs making up the U.S. response to the FCCC. The above-noted NAS recommendations were embodied in several sections of EPACT92. These sections included provisions to extend and expand energy efficiency standards, promote dissemination of energy-saving information, extend and expand research and development programs related to deployment of energy efficiency technologies, and authorize the Department of Energy (DOE) to evaluate cost-effective energy efficiency technologies. [88]

In December 1992, in response to the FCCC, the George H.W. Bush Administration issued the first U.S. climate action plan, [89] which called for an inventory of emissions and identified then-existing programs and activities that affect greenhouse gas emissions (GHG) as the core of the strategy for reducing emissions. These activities were dominated by research initiatives proposed in the 1991 National Energy Strategy, the Environmental Protection Agency's (EPA's) various pollution prevention, "green" initiatives begun in 1991, or were anticipated to result from the then recently-passed EPACT92. [90] Taken together, these programs and initiatives were consistent with guidance provided by the Intergovernmental Panel on Climate Change (IPCC) and formed the core of the George H. W. Bush Administration's "No Regrets" policy. [91] Underlying this approach, it appeared, was the presumption that uncertainties about global climate change were too great to justify actions beyond research except for so-called "no-regrets" initiatives justifiable on other grounds, such as selected energy efficiency and conservation measures.

The idea that the United States could meet modest CO_2 emission reduction goals at little or no cost underlies many of the global climate change initiatives during the George H. W. Bush and Clinton Administrations, including the George H. W. Bush Administration's "No Regrets" policy and 1992 Climate Action Plan, and the Clinton Administration's 1994 and 1997 Climate Action Plans. [92]

In fulfilling reporting requirements under FCCC, the Department of State issued the third U.S. climate report to the United Nations, entitled Climate Action Report 2002. [93] In it, the Bush Administration called for reducing GHG without interfering with economic growth and set out other general principles for a U.S. climate policy. [94] Taken together, these principles are consistent with the "no regrets" policy previously established by the George H.W. Bush Administration and expanded by the Clinton Administration.

In the Climate Action Report 2002, the Bush Administration committed to reducing greenhouse gas intensity (emissions per unit of GDP) by 18% (4% more than under existing policies) over 10 years through a combination of voluntary, incentive-based, and existing mandatory measures focused on energy efficiency and other measures. This was projected to attain a 4.5% reduction from forecast emissions in 2012. The Administration proposed this policy in place of the Kyoto Protocol, which it opposes due to concerns that it could raise energy prices and slow economic growth. Further, the Administration has stated its intent to support funding for energy efficiency and renewable energy programs at DOE and at the Global Environment Facility.

Also, the Energy Policy Act of 2005 (P.L. 109-58) contained several provisions to extend or expand energy efficiency standards programs. This includes energy efficiency standards for several types of equipment that were not previously covered, a variety of tax incentives, R&D program reauthorizations, and several other measures. [95] The American Council for an Energy Efficient Economy (ACEEE) estimates that by 2020, the energy efficiency provisions in EPACT would yield annual energy savings of about 2.6 Q per year and emission reductions of about 50 MMTC of carbon. [96] Relative to EIA projections, these figures would represent modest impacts of about 2% of total energy use and about 2.5% of total CO_2 emissions. [97]

Group of Eight (G8) Industrialized Nations. In its role as a member of the G8, [98] the United States has also expressed support for energy efficiency as a means to address greenhouse gas (GHG) emissions. In July 2005, the G8 issued The Gleneagles Communique, which included a Plan of Action on Climate Change, Clean Energy, and Sustainable Development. [99] The White House reported that President Bush and the G8 leaders agreed to speed the development and deployment of energy efficiency and other clean energy technologies to address climate change, air pollution, and energy security.

At its July 2006 Summit, the G8 issued the Saint Petersburg Plan of Action on Global Energy Security. [100] In the Plan, G8 commits to several goals, including "enhancing energy efficiency" and "addressing climate change." Specifically, Section III on "Enhancing Energy Efficiency and Energy Saving" indicates that the key goals are to reduce stress on energy infrastructure and decrease GHG emissions. To achieve those goals, the Plan calls for increased sharing of best practices, including practices for data collection and reporting, efficiency labeling, and efficiency standards. [101] Also, it encourages financial and tax incentives, governmental leadership by example, and actions at multilateral banks and GEF. This section of the Plan sets a focus on reducing losses in the transportation and energy production sectors. Further, it encourages incentives for energy efficiency in vehicles, biofuels, fuel cells, and air transportation. Overall, this section of the Plan encourages incentives for energy efficiency and energy conservation broadly.

U.S. Climate-Focused Energy Efficiency Programs

Domestic Programs. The U.S. Climate Change Technology Program (CCTP) encompasses an existing array of energy efficiency and other programs that support goals of the FCCC. Title XVI of EPACT expanded the statutory basis of CCTP. [102] Virtually all federal energy efficiency programs, including those at DOE, are treated as part of CCTP. [103]

DOE's August 2005 report U.S. Climate Change Technology Program — Technology Options for the Near and Long Term compiles information from multiple federal agencies on more than 80 technologies. [104] For these end-use energy efficiency and energy supply technologies, the report describes President Bush's initiatives and R&D goals for advancing technology development, but it does not estimate emissions saving potentials, as some previous DOE reports on the topic had done.

Foreign Assistance Programs. The Department of State, Foreign Operations, and Related Programs Appropriations Bill, 2006, provided $100 million for "energy conservation, energy efficiency, and clean energy" to reduce greenhouse gas (GHG) emissions in developing countries. [105] This funding continues support for this activity that has been provided for several consecutive years.

Appropriations Action in the Second Session. The action on the DOE Energy Efficiency Program and the EPA Climate Protection Program are described in detail above. [106] In addition, the Senate Appropriations Committee version of the Department of State, Foreign Operations, and Related Programs Appropriations Bill, 2007 (H.R. 5522; S.Rept. 109-277), would provide $180 million for energy efficiency and clean energy deployment activities to reduce GHG emissions in developing countries.

In January 2006, the Bush Administration announced its commitment to support the Asia Pacific Partnership (APP) for Clean Development and Climate to accelerate deployment of clean, energy efficient technologies. [107] Because of the lack of justification in the DOE FY2007 budget request, both the House and Senate appropriations committees declined to provide funding for APP in the FY2007 Energy and Water Development Appropriations bill (H.R. 5427). [108] However, both committees called on DOE to provide a justification for APP funds, so that they could take action in conference. [109] Further, the report of the Senate Appropriations Committee on the Department of State, Foreign Operations, and Related Programs Appropriations Bill, 2007, recommends $26 million for APP. [110]

California's Regulatory Action on Automobile CO_2 Emissions Could Promote Energy Efficiency

The State of California has launched a broad program to reduce greenhouse gas emissions (GHG), including a major focus on policies to encourage energy efficiency and renewable energy. As part of that effort, in September 2004, the California Air Resources Board (CARB) approved final rules (pursuant to AB1493) that would require car manufacturers to cut automobile carbon dioxide and other GHG emissions 22% by 2012. This could force automakers to increase vehicle fuel efficiency sharply. Although the rules take effect in 2006, new cars would not have to meet new standards until model year 2009.

However, an industry challenge to the California law and regulations was filed in U.S. District Court in Fresno, California. [111] The Alliance of Automobile Manufacturers joined several California car dealers in the law suit. The parties to the suit contend that an effort to regulate automobile CO_2 emissions is equivalent to regulating automobile fuel economy, but statutory authority to regulate fuel economy rests solely with the Department of Transportation's National Highway Traffic Safety Administration. [112]

Since the time that the lawsuit was filed, Oregon, Washington, and seven northeastern states have adopted automobile CO_2 emission regulations that parallel those in California. [113] Also, in April 2005, the Canadian government signed a "voluntary" agreement with automakers to reduce GHG by 5.3 million tons, or 17%, by 2010.

LEGISLATION

In the 109th Congress, more than 260 bills with provisions for energy efficiency or renewable energy have been introduced. A general description of the energy efficiency provisions in these bills, including those enacted into law, is available in CRS Report RL32860, Energy Efficiency and Renewable Energy Legislation in the 109th Congress, by Fred Sissine. The report also groups the bills by policy and issue areas, provides a table that identifies recent action on the bills, and discusses recent action on a month-by-month basis.

Appropriations Bills in the Second Session

H.R 5384 (Bonilla)

Agriculture, Rural Development, Food and Drug, Administration, and Related Agencies Appropriations Bill, 2007. Under Title III, Rural Development Programs, the bill would provide funding for the USDA Renewable Energy Program. The House approved $20 million and the Senate Appropriations Committee recommends $25 million. The Senate report language (p. 113) includes earmark recommendations. House Committee on Appropriations reported (H.Rept. 109-463) May 12, 2006, and reported Part II on May 16. Passed House, amended, May 23. Senate Committee on Appropriations reported (S.Rept. 109-266) June 22.

H.R. 5386 (C. Taylor)

Department of the Interior, Environment, and Related Agencies Appropriations Act, 2007. The House Committee on Appropriations reported (H.Rept. 109-465) May 15, 2006; recommending zero funding for EPA to support the Asia Pacific Partnership and $109.4 million for the EPA Climate Protection Program (CPP). [114] In House floor action, H.Amdt. 840 was adopted, adding $1.8 million to the CPP Energy Star Program. Also, H.Amdt. 849 was adopted, prohibiting use of the bill's appropriations in contravention of building energy efficiency performance requirements set by Executive Order 13123. Passed House, amended, May 18. The Senate Committee on Appropriations reported (S.Rept. 109-275) June 29, 2006; recommending $105.8 million.

H.R 5427 (Hobson)

Energy and Water Development Appropriations Act, 2007. Provides funding for the DOE Energy Efficiency Program. The details of House and Senate action are shown in Table 3. House Committee on Appropriations reported (H.Rept. 109-474) May 17, 2006, with amendments. Passed House, amended, May 24. Senate Committee on Appropriations ordered reported (S.Rept. 109-274) June 29.

H.R 5522 (Kolbe)

Department of State, Foreign Operations, and Related Programs Appropriations Bill, 2007. In the Senate version of the bill, under Title III, Bilateral Economic Assistance, the program for Development Assistance would include three types of support for renewable energy. First, the program for Energy, Biodiversity, and the Environment would, according to the Committee report (p. 65), provide $180 million "to support policies and programs in developing countries that promote energy efficiency, renewable energy, and cleaner energy technologies...." Also, $3 million would be provided for the U.S. Agency for International Development (USAID) partnership with DOE for the hydropower Clean Energy Technology Exports Initiative (CETEI). Second, under the USAID Development Assistance program, about $160 million would be provided (pp. 59-60) for Energy, Biodiversity, and Other Environment programs for Africa ($73 million), East Asia/Pacific ($28 million), Near East ($2 million), South Asia ($18 million), and Western Hemisphere ($52 million). Third, under Other Bilateral Economic Assistance, the bill would provide $26 million for the Asia Pacific Partnership, and further specifies (p. 73) that the "... Partnership activities will be coordinated with existing efforts to promote clean energy export and market development initiatives." House Committee on Appropriations reported (H.Rept. 109-486) June 5, 2006, with amendments. Passed House, amended, June 9. Senate Committee on Appropriations reported (S.Rept. 109-277) July 10.

Energy Policy Act of 2005 (EPACT, P.L. 109-58)

The enacted version (H.Rept. 109-190) authorizes or reauthorizes several energy efficiency and conservation programs. It also establishes several new commercial and consumer product efficiency standards, sets new goals for energy efficiency in federal facilities and fleets, broadens the Energy Star products program, expands programs for hydrogen fuel cell buses, and extends daylight savings. However, it does not include Senate-proposed provisions for oil conservation and a broader range of legislated equipment efficiency standards. Conference reported (H.Rept. 109-190) July 27, 2005. Signed into law August 8.

Other Public Laws of the 109th Congress

P.L. 109-54 (H.R. 2361)

Department of the Interior, Environment, and Related Agencies Appropriations Bill, 2006. The conference bill includes $112.5 million for EPA's Climate Protection Program (energy efficiency) — $93.5 million under the Office of Environmental Programs and Management (EPM) and $19.0 million under the Office of Science and Technology (S&T). Conference reported (H.Rept. 109-188) July 26, 2005. Signed into law August 2.

Note: Four other public laws make appropriations for energy efficiency programs. P.L. 109-97 (H.R. 2744) makes appropriations for grant and loan (§9006) programs at the Department of Agriculture; P.L. 109-102 (H.R. 3057, §585[a]) makes appropriations for the Department of State's climate change programs in developing countries, including $100 million that "should be made available to directly promote and deploy energy conservation, energy efficiency, and renewable and clean energy technologies"; P.L. 109-103 (H.R. 2419) makes appropriations for the DOE energy efficiency (energy conservation R&D and grant) programs; and P.L. 109-108 (H.R. 2862, §618 and §619) directs several federal agencies to certify that telecommuting opportunities have increased over the previous year and several other agencies to certify that telecommuting opportunities are available to 100% of the eligible workforce. Failure to certify would cause agencies to risk forfeiting $5 million. [115]

P.L. 109-171 (S. 1932)

Deficit Reduction Act of 2005. Section 1301 amends section 9006(f) of the Farm Security Act of 2002 to set a limit of $3 million in FY2007 funding for the USDA Commodity Credit Corporation to carry out renewable energy and energy efficiency projects. Section 1402 terminates FY2007 funding authorization for the USDA Value-Added Producer Program (created by section 6401 of the Farm Security Act of 2002) to provide grants to renewable energy and energy efficiency projects. Conference reported (H.Rept. 109-362) December 19, 2005. Signed into law February 8, 2006.

P.L. 109-59 (H.R. 3)

Transportation Equity Act. Sections related to energy efficiency and conservation include 1121, high occupancy vehicle (HOV) facilities; 1307, magnetic levitation transportation; 1807, nonmotorized transportation pilot program; 1808, additions to congestion mitigation and air quality (CMAQ); 1952, congestion relief; 1954, bicycle transportation and pedestrian walkways; 3005, metropolitan transportation planning; 3016, national research and technology programs; 3045, national fuel cell bus technology development program; 4149, office of intermodalism; 5301, intelligent transportation systems; 5502, congestion relief research initiative; 6001, transportation planning; and 9002, study of high speed rail. House bill introduced February 9, 2005; referred to Committee on Transportation and Infrastructure. Conference reported (H.Rept. 109-203) July 28, 2005. Signed into law August 10.

REFERENCES

[1] For more details, see "DOE Budget, FY2007" and Table 3. Also, the DOE FY2007 budget request document is online at [http://www.cfo.doe.gov/budget/index.htm].

[2] More details about earmarks for DOE's energy efficiency programs can be found in CRS Report RL33294, DOE Budget Earmarks: A Selective Look at Energy Efficiency and Renewable Energy R&D Programs, by Fred Sissine.

[3] For more details, see "EPA Budget, FY2007" and Table 2, below.

[4] For more details, see the "Legislation" and "Climate Change" sections below.

[5] A list of all energy efficiency bills introduced in the 109th Congress is provided in CRS Report RL32860, Energy Efficiency and Renewable Energy Legislation in the 109thCongress, by Fred Sissine.

[6] Also referred to as the "take-back" effect, the rebound effect is discussed in the following section, "Measuring the Rebound Effect."

[7] This equipment is selected and installed by millions of consumers and companies, which calls for a different approach to measurement than that for energy supplies.

[8] Evaluation research is an empirical social science discipline that originated in the 1960s with a focus on the use of control and treatment groups to measure the effects of education, health, and other social programs. As broad-based energy programs emerged in the late 1970s and early 1980s, these techniques began to be applied to many energy programs.

[9] Evaluations of energy efficiency and energy conservation programs have continued, but they are focused mostly on effects at the state or local level. The International Energy Program Evaluation Conference is at the center of this continuing effort. See abstracts of evaluation papers from its 2005 conference at [http://www.iepec.org/].

[10] Prominent examples are U.S. DOE, Oak Ridge National Laboratory (ORNL), Past Efforts and Future Directions for Evaluating State Energy Conservation Programs (ORNL-6113), 1985; Office of State and Local Assistance Programs, Institutional Conservation Program Evaluation Project, 1986; and ORNL, National Impacts of the Weatherization Assistance Program in Single-Family and Small Multifamily Dwellings (ORNL/CON-326), 1993.

[11] This is true for virtually all R&D programs, not just for energy efficiency R&D programs. The Bush Administration has launched an effort under the President's Management Agenda to develop methods for assessing the impacts of applied R&D programs, including the Energy Efficiency Program at DOE. The National Academy of Sciences has published reports in this area, including Energy Research at DOE: Was It Worth It? Energy Efficiency and Fossil Energy Research 1978 to 2000, 2001, at [http://darwin.nap.edu/books/ 0309074487/html/9.html], and Prospective Evaluation of Applied Energy Research and Development at DOE (Phase One): A First Look Forward, 2005, at [http://darwin.nap.edu/ books/0309096049/html/70.html].

[12] National Academy of Sciences, Energy Use: The Human Dimension, Chapter 4, "Individuals and Households as Energy Users," 1984, p. 60.

[13] NAS, Energy Use, p. 61.

[14] For more information, see Lee Schipper, "On the Rebound: The Interaction of Energy Efficiency, Energy Use and Economic Activity: An Introduction," Energy Policy, vol. 28, 2000, p. 351-353. Also see CRS Report RS20981, Energy Efficiency and the Rebound Effect: Does Increasing Efficiency Decrease Demand? by Frank Gottron.

[15] DOE, Energy Conservation Trends: Understanding the Factors That Affect Conservation Gains in the U.S. Economy (DOE/PE-0092), September 1989.

[16] DOE, Energy Conservation Trends: Understanding the Factors Affecting Conservation Gains and Their Implications for Policy Development (DOE/PO-0034), April 1995, 50 p.

[17] A quad is a quadrillion Btus (British thermal units).

[18] DOE noted that the areas of rising demand included increased use of air conditioning in the residential sector, greater use of air conditioning and office equipment (e.g., computers, printers, and copiers) in the commercial sector, a decline in the ratio of load-to-vehicle weight for heavy trucks in the transportation sector, and a shift from cars to light trucks in consumer vehicle choices.

[19] DOE, Energy Conservation Trends, 1995, p. 33-35.

[20] EIA, Measuring Energy Efficiency In The United States' Economy: A Beginning, October 1995, 91 p., at [http://www.eia.doe.gov/emeu/efficiency/ee_report_html.htm].

[21] EIA, p.71.

[22] EIA, Measuring Energy Efficiency, pp. vii and 4.

[23] In discussing the behavioral aspect as an intervening variable in measuring energy efficiency, EIA notes that a consumer may decide to reallocate the energy savings to an increased level of service, such as a higher heating temperature in winter. This behavioral phenomena is know as the "rebound effect," as previously discussed.

[24] EIA notes that for any given service, energy intensity is inversely related to energy efficiency; pp. 3-4.

[25] EIA, pp. 5-6.

[26] EIA, p. 71.

[27] EIA, p. 71.

[28] EIA's Energy Efficiency Measurement Discussion was last updated in February 2003 and is available online at [http://www.eia.doe.gov/emeu/efficiency/measure_discussion.htm].

[29] EIA, Energy Efficiency Measurement Discussion, section on "Energy Intensity as a Common Surrogate for Energy Efficiency."

[30] EIA also notes that there is a "best practice approach" that can be used for comparing the efficiency of a current or average production activity with the "best practice" that could be used. This approach is most appropriately applied to single production process or single company.

[31] The "market-basket (of energy services) approach" is a bottom-up approach, in which each category of service is controlled relative to its share in the index. The "comprehensive approach" works from the top-down, starting with the broadest measures of energy use and then removing effects from behavior, weather, and structure. The "factorial decomposition approach" takes energy use and separates it into activity, structural, and intensity effects, measuring each by holding the other two constant. This technique is used by the International Energy Agency in its publication Indicators of Energy Use and Efficiency. The "Divisia index approach" separates time trends into different factors, such as structure and intensity.

[32] This is particularly important for electricity, where large amounts of heat are lost in the combustion of fossil fuels to generate power. However, it is also true for a fuel refinery, where certain amounts of energy are used to operate the machinery that drives the chemical processes. Primary energy use is related to the concept of "full fuel cycle" energy use.

[33] This is usually the easiest measure of use, shown on home electricity and natural gas meters.

[34] With an economic measure, EIA said it does not matter if there is a shift from electricity to natural gas or vice versa because a decrease in the cost of one fuel is likely

to be counterbalanced by an increase in the other. Thus, in this view, although site energy use may decline relative to primary energy use, the expenditures would remain relatively level.
[35] Detailed descriptions of DOE programs appear in DOE's FY2007 Congressional Budget Request, DOE/CF-004, vol. 3, February 2006, available at [http://www.mbe.doe.gov/budget/07budget/Content/Volumes/vol_3_ES.pdf].
[36] In FY2006, as part of a restructuring of the appropriations committees, Congress merged appropriations accounts for the DOE Energy Efficiency Program, which had previously been under the Department of the Interior and Related Agencies Appropriations Bill, with the appropriations accounts for the DOE Renewable Energy Program under the Energy and Water Development Appropriations Bill. As a result, appropriations for some subprograms, such as Hydrogen and Program Management, of the Renewable Energy Program are commingled with those for the Energy Efficiency Program and are no longer reported separately. In place of the former totals for the Energy Efficiency Program, this report (see Table 3) now shows a subtotal of appropriations for all of the energy efficiency technology subprograms, namely Hydrogen, Fuel Cells, Vehicles, Buildings, and Industrial Technologies.
[37] DOE, Pacific Northwest Laboratory, An Analysis of Federal Incentives Used to Stimulate Energy Production (PNL-2410 REV II, UC-59), February 1980, 374 p. See also selected publications by Warren Donnelly, CRS.
[38] DOE, Office of the Chief Financial Officer, Budget Authority History Table by Appropriation, FY1978 through FY2006 Request (table), June 7, 2005.
[39] The study is available on the NAPA website at [http://www.napawash.org/Pubs/EERE% 20NAPA%20Rpt%20Sept%2004.htm].
[40] Information about the new management structure and other aspects of EERE are available on the DOE website at [http://www1.eere.energy.gov/office_eere/].
[41] The report says that most of the estimated benefits were attributed to three relatively modest building sector projects conducted from the late 1970s into the 1990s. National Research Council. Energy Research at DOE: Was It Worth It? (Energy Efficiency and Fossil Energy Research 1978 to 2000), Executive Summary, p. 6., at [http://darwin.nap.edu/ execsumm_pdf/10165.pdf]
[42] NRC, Energy Research at DOE, p. 7.
[43] The NRC report is available at [http://darwin.nap.edu/books/0309074487/html/79.html]. NRC, Energy Research at DOE (Overall Findings and Recommendations), p. 67.
[44] DOE says these awards are known as the "Oscars of Innovation." DOE, FY2006 Congressional Budget Request (Interior and Related Agencies), February 2005, vol. 7, p. 217.
[45] The full report is available on the RFF website at [http://www.rff.org/Documents/ RFF-DP-04-19REV.pdf].
[46] DOE, FY2007 Congressional Budget Request (Energy Supply and Conservation), vol. 3, p. 17-18.
[47] DOE, FY2007 Budget Request, p. 19.
[48] DOE, FY2006 Congressional Budget Request (Interior and Related Agencies), February 2005, vol. 7, p. 217.

[49] The White House, State of the Union: American Competitiveness Initiative, January 31, 2006, at [http://www.whitehouse.gov/news/releases/2006/01/20060131-5.html].
[50] The White House, State of the Union: the Advanced Energy Initiative, January 31, 2006, at [http://www.whitehouse.gov/news/releases/2006/01/20060131-6.html].
[51] DOE, Department of Energy Requests $23.6 million for FY2007, press release, February 6, 2006, at [http://www.doe.gov/news/3150.htm].
[52] U.S. Executive Office of the President, Budget of the United States Government, Fiscal Year 2007, Appendix, p. 390. Also see DOE, FY2007 Congressional Budget Request: Budget Highlights, p. 41.
[53] U.S. Executive Office of the President, Office of Science and Technology Policy, Domestic Policy Council, American Competitiveness Initiative Leading the World in Innovation, February 2006, p. 13, at [http://www.house.gov/science/hot/Competitiveness/ aci06-booklet.pdf].
[54] U.S. Congress, House, Committee on Science, Hearing on Fiscal Year 2007 Federal R&D Budget, Testimony of John Marburger III (Director of the Office of Science and Technology Policy), Feb. 15, 2006, p. 1-2. His statement also covered the ACI initiative; see [http://www.house.gov/science/hearings/full06/Feb15/marburger.pdf]. For additional information on Energy Conservation Programs, see [http://www.eere.energy.gov/].
[55] U.S. Congress, House, Committee on Appropriations, Energy and Water Appropriations Bill, 2007, H.Rept. 109-474, May 19, 2006, p. 74-81, at [http://frwebgate.access.gpo.gov/ cgi-bin/getdoc.cgi?dbname=109_cong_reports&docid =f:hr474.109.pdf]
[56] H.Rept. 109-474, p. 73.
[57] H.Rept. 109-474, pp. 74-75.
[58] H.Rept. 109-474, pp. 67-68.
[59] U.S. Congress, Senate, Committee on Appropriations, Energy and Water Appropriations Bill, 2007, S.Rept. 109-274, June 29, 2006, pp. 114-122, at [http://frwebgate.access. gpo.gov/cgi-bin/getdoc.cgi?dbname=109_cong_reports&docid =f:sr274.109.pdf].
[60] S.Rept. 109-274, pp. 118-119.
[61] S.Rept. 109-274, p. 119.
[62] U.S. Environmental Protection Agency (EPA), 2007 Annual Performance Plan and Congressional Justification, Climate Protection Program, S&T-23 to S&T-25, EPM-2, and EPM-35 to EPM-40.
[63] Table 2 shows that standards for three products would be set by DOE rulemaking.
[64] DOE, Energy Conservation Standards Activities: Submitted Pursuant to Section 141 of the Energy Policy Act of 2005 and to the Conference Report (109-275) to the FY 2006 Energy and Water Development Appropriations Act, January 2006, 85 p. The schedule is posted on the DOE website at [http://www.eere.energy.gov/buildings/appliance _standards/2006_schedule_setting.html].
[65] The report describes the reasons for each delay and DOE's plan for issuing new or amended standards.
[66] For more information on this topic, see CRS Report RS20935, Energy Efficiency in Congressional Buildings, by Fred Sissine.

[67] EIA, Electric Utility Demand Side Management 1997, Executive Summary, at [http://www.eia.doe.gov/cneaf/electricity/dsm/dsm_sum.html].

[68] In response, some states, such as California, included provisions for energy efficiency and conservation in their restructuring legislation. For example, California's law (A.B. 1890, Article 7) placed a "public goods" charge on all electricity bills that provides about $300 million per year for "cost effective" energy efficiency and conservation programs directed by the California Energy Commission.

[69] EIA, Electric Power Annual 2004, November 2005, Table 9.6, p. 57.

[70] U.S. DOE, Lawrence Berkeley National Laboratory, California Consumers Kept Lights on During Electricity Crisis by Conserving and Investing in Efficient Equipment (Report #49733), May 2002, at [http://www.lbl.gov/Science-Articles/Archive/EETD-Goldmanelectricity.html].

[71] EPA has posted the Plan at [http://www.epa.gov/cleanenergy/actionplan/report.htm].

[72] NPC has posted the report at [http://www.npc.org/].

[73] The ACEEE report is available at [http://www.aceee.org/energy/efnatgas-study.htm].

[74] See [http://energy.senate.gov/conference/conference.cfm].

[75] The report is available at [http://eetd.lbl.gov/ea/ems/reports/56756.pdf].

[76] In 1975, Congress enacted the Energy Policy and Conservation Act (P.L. 94-163), in which Title V required that automotive manufacturers selling cars in the United States increase the corporate average fuel economy (CAFE) of their new-car fleet annually, from 18.0 miles per gallon (mpg) in model year (MY) 1978 until reaching 27.5 mpg in model year (MY) 1985. A parallel standard for light trucks started at 17.2 mpg in MY1979, rising to 20.7 mpg by MY1991.

[77] NHTSA, New Light Truck Fuel Standards to Save 10.7 Billion Gallons of Fuel, Mar. 29, 2006, at [http://www.nhtsa.dot.gov/portal/site/nhtsa/menuitem.d0b5a45b55bfbe582f57529cdba046a0/].

[78] For more on CAFE standards, see CRS Report RL33413, Automobile and Light Truck Fuel Economy: The CAFE Standards, by Brent Yacobucci and Robert Bamberger.

[79] EIA, Monthly Energy Review (June 2006), Table 1.9, p. 17, at [http://www.eia.doe.gov/emeu/mer/overview.html]

[80] The CBO report is available at [http://www.cbo.gov/showdoc.cfm?index=4917&sequence=0].

[81] The report is online at [http://www.ornl.gov/sci/eere/cef/].

[82] The BAU case for 2020 is somewhat lower than that for the EIA Reference Case, because it assumes some technological improvements that EIA does not include.

[83] EIA's projection appears under the Reference Case, Table A18. Carbon Dioxide Emissions. Also, the factor of 3.67 was used to convert tons of CO_2 to tons of carbon.

[84] In 1991, the Intergovernmental Panel on Climate Change (IPCC) issued a report providing guidance to nations considering action on global climate change. It recommended actions that were beneficial for reasons other than climate change and justifiable in their own right (e.g., energy efficiency), economically efficient and cost-effective (especially those focused on market-mechanisms), and able to serve multiple social, economic, and environmental purposes.

[85] For more information about U.S. climate change policy, see CRS Report RL30024, Global Climate Change Policy: Cost, Competitiveness, and Comprehensiveness, by Larry B. Parker and John E. Blodgett.

[86] National Academy of Sciences, Policy Implications of Greenhouse Warming, (Washington, DC: National Academy Press, 1991), p. 73.

[87] NAS also called for incorporating greenhouse warming as a factor in future energy planning, and studying and eventually implementing "full social cost pricing" of energy.

[88] It should be noted, however, that typically the programs are relatively specific, not broad authorizations; that for many the benefit of reducing greenhouse gases is a "bonus" in achieving other goals (e.g., "substantially reduce environmental pollutants, including greenhouse gases..." [EPACT92, sec. 1608])

[89] U.S. Department of State, National Action Plan for Global Climate Change (Publication 10026), December 1992.

[90] The primary reasons for the DOE and EPA programs were to conserve energy and to reduce air pollution — any global climate change benefits would be a bonus. Thus exemplifying "no regrets" — the action is one that is justified for other reasons. As codified by the 1992 National Action Plan, the combination of DOE and EPA programs were projected to hold U.S. greenhouse gas emissions at near their 1990 levels in the year 2000. Those programs were not able to fulfill that objective.

[91] On the "no regrets" policy of the George H.W. Bush Administration, see C. Boyden Gray and David B. Rivkin, Jr., "A 'No Regrets' Environmental Policy," Foreign Policy, summer 1991, pp. 47-65.

[92] See CRS Report RL30024, Global Climate Change Policy, by Larry B. Parker and John E. Blodgett.

[93] U.S. Department of State, U.S. Climate Action Report: The United States of America's Third National Communication Under the United Nations Framework Convention on Climate Change, May 2002, at [http://yosemite.epa.gov/oar/globalwarming.nsf/content/ResourceCenterPublicationsUSClimateActionReport.html].

[94] The other principles are establish a goal to stabilize emissions, create flexibility to allow for new findings, provide market-based incentives, incorporate technological advances, and promote global participation.

[95] These provisions are described in the above section on the Energy Policy Act of 2005.

[96] ACEEE's estimate of savings is available at [http://www.aceee.org/energy/0510confsvg. pdf].

[97] For 2020, EIA's Annual Energy Outlook 2006 reference case estimates are 120.6 quads of energy use and 7,119 MMTC of CO_2 (or 1,942 MMTC of carbon).

[98] The G8 includes the United States, four members of the European Union (France, Germany, Italy, and United Kingdom), Canada, Japan, and the Russian Federation. Together, these nations represent two-thirds of the world economy. The G8 convenes an annual economic and political summit meeting with the heads of the respective governments.

[99] After its annual summit each year, the G8 issues a policy document that may include energy-related provisions. The G8 Summit in 2005 did include such a document with energy policy-related provisions. The Gleneagles documents can be obtained at [http://www.g8.gov.uk/servlet/Front?pagename=OpenMarket/Xcelerate/ShowPage&c=P age&cid=1119518698846].

[100] The G8 Saint Petersburg Plan is available at [http://en.g8russia.ru/docs/11-print.html].

[101]This includes the International Energy Agency's initiative to promote efficiency standards for standby power devices.

[102]A summary of the provisions in Title XVI is available in CRS Report RL33302, Energy Policy Act of 2005: Summary and Analysis of Enacted Provisions, by Mark Holt and Carol Glover.

[103]At least four appropriation programs — for DOE, EPA, USDA, and the Department of State — provide funding for energy efficiency programs that contribute to the reduction of greenhouse gas emissions.

[104]The report is available at [http://www.climatetechnology.gov/library/2005/tech-options/index.htm].

[105]This funding provision is in Section 585(a) of P.L. 109-102 (H.R. 3057).

[106]USDA also has a program for energy efficiency and renewable energy, but its funding is on a much smaller scale, ranging from $10 million to $20 million per year. For more about the USDA program, see CRS Report RL33588, Renewable Energy Policy: Tax Credit, Budget, and Regulatory Issues, by Fred Sissine.

[107]APP participants include Australia, China, India, Japan, Korea, and the United States. The APP initiative appears to be a followup to the U.S. commitments under The Gleneagles Communique.

[108]For the same reason, the House Committee on Appropriations recommended zero funding at EPA for APP (H.R. 5386, H.Rept. 109-465).

[109]H.Rept. 109-474, p. 69. S.Rept. 109-274, pp. 111-112. In its report, the Senate Appropriations Committee further directed DOE to fund APP from within available funds, with one-third from the Office of Policy and International Affairs, one-third from the Office of Science (Climate Change Account), and one-third from the Office of Energy Efficiency and Renewable Energy. The Senate report also directed APP to work with the Clean Energy Technology Exports Program.

[110]The recommendation appears under "Other Bilateral Economic Assistance," and the reference to exports appears on p. 73. Also, the report specifies that APP be coordinated with clean energy export and market development initiatives.

[111]Alliance of Automobile Manufacturers, Automakers and Dealers Cite Federal Law, Marketplace Principles, in Challenging Carbon Dioxide Law, press release, Dec. 7, 2004,at [http://www.autoalliance.org/archives/000163.html].

[112]Also, on December 21, 2005, CARB sent a letter to EPA requesting a waiver of federal preemption of state regulation of GHG; see [http://www.arb.ca.gov/cc/docs/waiver.pdf].

[113]The seven states are Connecticut, Maine, Massachusetts, New Jersey, New York, Rhode Island, and Vermont.

[114]CPP primarily supports energy efficiency deployment in transportation, buildings, and industry sectors.

[115]More details about these laws and other bills are described in CRS Report RL32860, Energy Efficiency and Renewable Energy Legislation in the 109th Congress, by Fred Sissine.

Congressional Hearings, Reports, and Documents

(An extensive list of hearings appears in CRS Report RL32860, Energy Efficiency and Renewable Energy Legislation in the 109th Congress, by Fred Sissine. Also, testimony by officials of DOE's Office of Energy Efficiency and Renewable Energy (EERE) at many hearings of the 109th Congress are listed on EERE's website at [http://www1.eere.energy.gov/office_eere/congressional_test.html].)

For Additional Reading

American Council for an Energy-Efficient Economy. Proceedings from the ACEEE 2004 Summer Study on Energy Efficiency in Buildings. Washington, 2004. (10 v.)

ACEEE's Green Book Online: Guide to Cars and Trucks, Model Year 2006. Highlights at [http://www.greenercars.com/bestof.html].

Cato Institute. The High Costs of Federal Energy Efficiency Standards for Residential Appliances. (Policy Analysis No. 504) 2003. 15 p.

Government Accountability Office (GAO). Research and Development: Lessons Learned from Research Could Benefit FreedomCAR Initiative. (GAO -028101) 2002. 50 p.

National Association of Manufacturers (NAM). Efficiency and Innovation in U.S. Manufacturing Energy Use. 2005. 37 p. [http://www.fypower.org/pdf/Mfg_NAM_ASE.pdf]

National Association of Regulatory Utility Commissioners (NARUC). AGA and NRDC Release Energy Efficiency (Conservation Tariff) Joint Statement. 2004. 4 p. [http://www.naruc.org/displayindustryarticle.cfm?articlenbr=21073&startrec=1]

National Research Council. Energy Research at DOE: Was It Worth It? (Energy Efficiency and Fossil Energy Research 1978 to 2000). 2001. 224 p. [http://www.nap.edu/books/0309074487/html/]

– Effectiveness and Impact of Corporate Average Fuel Economy (CAFE) Standards. 2001. 184 p.

Rocky Mountain Institute. Winning the Oil Endgame: Innovation for Profits, Jobs, and Security. 2004. 306 p. [https://www.rmi.org/store/p12details4772.php]

U.S. Department of Energy. Energy Information Administration. Impacts of Modeled Recommendations of the National Commission on Energy Policy.

[Report on CAFE fuel economy] (SR/OIAF/2005-02) April 2005. 79 p. [http://www.eia.doe.gov/oiaf/servicerpt/bingaman/]

– Interlaboratory Working Group. Scenarios for a Clean Energy Future. (ORNL/CON-476) 2000. 350 p. [http://www.ornl.gov/sci/eere/cef/]

– State Energy Advisory Board. Homeland Security: Safeguarding America's Future with Energy Efficiency and Renewable Energy. (DOE/EE-0272) 2000. 26 p. [http://www.steab.org/]

U.S. Environmental Protection Agency. U.S. Climate Action Report 2002. 2002. 260 p. [http://yosemite.epa.gov/oar/globalwarming.nsf/content/ResourceCenterPublicationsUSClimateActionReport.html].

– Investing in Our Future: Energy Star and Other Voluntary Programs 2004 Annual Report. September 2005. 54 p. [http://www.energystar.gov/ia/news/downloads/annual_report2004.pdf]

U.S. Government Accountability Office (GAO). Electricity Markets: Consumers Could Benefit from Demand Programs, But Challenges Remain (GAO-04-844) August 2004. 68 p. [http://www.gao.gov/new.items/d04844.pdf]

CRS Reports

CRS Report RL33294. *DOE Budget Earmarks: A Selected Look at Energy Efficiency and Renewable Energy R&D Programs*, by Fred Sissine.

CRS Report RL32860. *Energy Efficiency and Renewable Energy Legislation in the 109th Congress*, by Fred Sissine.

CRS Report RL30414. *Global Climate Change: The Role for Energy Efficiency*, by Fred Sissine.

CRS Report RS20298. *Sport Utility Vehicles, Mini-Vans, and Light Trucks: An Overview of Fuel Economy and Emissions Standards*, by Brent Yacobucci.

CRS Report RL32251. *Tax Incentives for Alternative Fuel and Advanced Technology Vehicles*, by Brent Yacobucci.

Websites

Alliance to Save Energy. Many resources on energy efficiency. [http://www.ase.org/]

American Council for an Energy-Efficient Economy (ACEEE). Extensive listing of websites on energy efficiency. [http://www.aceee.org/]

National Association of State Energy Offices. [http://www.naseo.org/]

Tax Incentives Assistance Project. Resources for energy efficiency incentives in P.L. 109-58 (H.R. 6). [http://www.energytaxincentives.org/]

U.S. Council for Automotive Research (USCAR). FreedomCAR. [http://www.uscar.org/freedomcar/index.htm]

U.S. Department of Energy. Energy Efficiency and Renewable Energy Network. [http://www.eere.energy.gov/]

U.S. Department of Energy. FY2007 Congressional Budget Request. [http://www.cfo.doe.gov/budget/07budget/Content/Volumes/vol_3_ES.pdf]

U.S. Department of Energyand U.S. Environmental Protection Agency. Fuel Economy. [http://www.fueleconomy.gov/]

U.S. Lawrence Berkeley Laboratory. Center for Building Science. [http://eetd.lbl.gov/]

U.S. Environmental Protection Agency. EPA FY2006 Annual Performance Plan and Congressional Justification (S&T-24; EPM-2, 34). [http://www.epa.gov/ocfopage/budget/2007/2007cj.htm]

U.S. Environmental Protection Agency. Energy Star Programs. [http://www.energystar.gov/]

Table 4. DOE Energy Efficiency Budget for FY2005-FY2007 (selected programs, $ millions)

	FY2005 Appn.	FY2006 Appn.	FY2006 Request	FY2006 House	FY2007 Senate Cmte	Senate-House Percent Change
HYDROGEN TECH.	166.8	155.6	195.8	195.8	189.9	-3.0%
Fuel Cell Tech.	81.9	67.8	96.6	96.6	85.4	-11.6%
VEHICLE TECH.	161.3	182.1	166.0	172.5	180.0	4.4%
Hybrid and Electric	44.1	44.0	50.8	50.8	——d	——
Advanced Combustion	48.5	45.6	46.7	53.2	——	——
Materials Technology	36.0	35.3	29.8	29.8	——	——
Fuels Technology	12.4	13.7	13.8	13.8	——	——
Technology Introduction	4.9	6.3	11.0	11.0	15.0	36.0%
Clean Cities	10.6	7.9	4.4	5.0	6.4	27.9%
BUILDING TECH.	65.2	69.3	77.3	80.0	95.3	19.1%
Res. & Commercial Bldgs	21.9	18.3	24.4	24.4	——	——
Emerging Technologies	31.1	33.1	32.8	32.8	——	——
Tech. Valid. & Mkt. Intro.	0.0	0.0	8.2	8.2	——	——
Rebuild America	8.6	3.8	2.5	2.5	——	——
Energy Star	3.7	5.9	5.8	5.8	——	——
INDUSTRIAL TECH.	73.4	56.9	45.6	51.6	47.6	-7.8%
Ind. of the Future, Specific	37.4	24.2	17.0	21.0	——	——
Ind. of the Future, Cross.	32.3	28.9	28.6	28.6	——	——
Combustion, Robotics, Sensors	4.5	3.1	5.4	5.4	——	——
Industrial Tech. Assist.	15.1	14.4	12.9	12.9	——	——
DISTRIB. ENERGY RES.a	59.1	0.0	0.0	0.0	——	——
FED. ENERGY MGMT	19.9	19.2	16.9	18.9	16.9	-10.6%
WEATHERIZATION	325.5	316.9	225.0	335.4	266.4	-20.6%
Weatherization Program	228.2	242.6	164.2	268.0	200.0	-25.4%
State Energy Grants	44.2	35.6	49.5	49.5	49.5	0.0%
State Energy Activities	2.3	0.5	0.0	0.0	——	——
Gateway Deploymentb	33.9	25.4	0.0	0.0	——	——

Table 4. DOE Energy Efficiency Budget for FY2005-FY2007 (selected programs, $ millions) (Continued)

	FY2005 Appn.	FY2006 Appn.	FY2006 Request	FY2006 House	FY2007 Senate Cmte	Senate-House Percent Change
Inventions	3.9	3.0	0.0	2.0	——	——
PROGRAM MGMT	115.1	111.9	102.0	102.0	101.9	-8.8%
Prior Year Balances	-5.3	——	——	——	——	——
EERE, TOTALa	1,234.3	1,173.8	1,176.4	1,319.4	1,385.5	5.0%
EFFICIENCY R&D, SUB.c	466.6	463.9	484.7	499.9	512.8	2.6%
GRANTS, SUBTOTAL	272.3	278.2	213.7	317.5	249.5	-21.4%
EE EARMARKS, SUB.	34.0	76.4	0.0	26.1	15.8	-39.6%

Sources: DOE FY2007 Budget Request, vol. 3, February 2006; H.Rept. 109-474; S.Rept. 109-274.

a. Funding for Distributed Energy was moved to the Office of Electricity Delivery and Energy Reliability.

b. The request would terminate Gateway Deployment and movesome subprograms to other Programs.

c. Efficiency R&D Subtotal includes Hydrogen, Fuel Cells, Vehicles, Buildings, and Industrial Technologies.

d. Information about many subprograms was not available in the Senate report.

In: Energy Policy: Issues, Actions and Consequences
Editor: Quentin V. Harris
ISBN 978-1-60692-225-5

Chapter 3

ENERGY INDEPENDENCE AND SECURITY ACT OF 2007: A SUMMARY OF MAJOR PROVISIONS*

Fred Sissine

ABSTRACT

The Energy Independence and Security Act (P.L. 110-140, H.R. 6) is an omnibus energy policy law that consists mainly of provisions designed to increase energy efficiency and the availability of renewable energy. This report describes the key provisions of the enacted law, summarizes the legislative action on H.R. 6, and provides a summary of the provisions under each of the titles in the law.

The highlights of key provisions enacted into law are as follows:

- Corporate Average Fuel Economy (CAFE). The law sets a target of 35 miles per gallon for the combined fleet of cars and light trucks by model year 2020.
- Renewable Fuels Standard (RFS). The law sets a modified standard that starts at 9.0 billion gallons in 2008 and rises to 36 billion gallons by 2022.
- Energy Efficiency Equipment Standards. The adopted bill includes a variety of new standards for lighting and for residential and commercial appliance equipment. The equipment includes residential refrigerators, freezers, refrigerator-freezers, metal halide lamps, and commercial walk-in coolers and freezers.
- Repeal of Oil and Gas Tax Incentives. The enacted law includes repeal of two tax subsidies in order to offset the estimated cost to implement the CAFE provision.

The two most controversial provisions of H.R. 6 that were not included in the enacted law were the proposed Renewable Energy Portfolio Standard (RPS) and most of the proposed tax provisions, which included repeal of tax subsidies for oil and gas and new incentives for energy efficiency and renewable energy.

---

* This is an edited, excerpted and augmented edition of a CRS Report RL34294, dated December 21, 2007 publication.

INTRODUCTION

The Energy Independence and Security Act (P.L. 110-140, H.R. 6) is an omnibus energy policy law that consists mainly of provisions designed to increase energy efficiency and the availability of renewable energy. This report describes the key provisions of the enacted law, summarizes the legislative action on H.R. 6, and provides a summary of the provisions under each of the titles in the law.

Many analysts in the CRS Resources, Science, and Industry Division contributed to this report; their names and contact information are located on the back of the summary page.

KEY PROVISIONS

Provisions Included

The three key provisions enacted in P.L. 110-140 are the Corporate Average Fuel Economy (CAFE) Standards, the Renewable Fuel Standard (RFS), and the appliance/lighting efficiency standards.

Corporate Average Fuel Economy (CAFE) Standards. The law sets a target of 35 miles per gallon for the combined fleet of cars and light trucks by model year 2020. Also, a fuel economy program is established for medium- and heavy-duty trucks, and a separate fuel economy standard is created for work trucks. (For more details on issues related to the CAFE provision, see CRS Report RL33982, Corporate Average Fuel Economy (CAFE): A Comparison of Selected Legislation in the 110th Congress, by Brent D. Yacobucci and Robert Bamberger, and CRS Report RL33413, Automobile and Light Truck Fuel Economy: The CAFE Standards, by Brent D. Yacobucci and Robert Bamberger.)

Renewable Fuel Standard (RFS). The law sets a modified standard that starts at 9.0 billion gallons of renewable fuel in 2008 and rises to 36 billion gallons by 2022. Of the latter total, 21 billion gallons is required to be obtained from cellulosic ethanol and other advanced biofuels. (For more details on issues related to the RFS provision, see CRS Report RL34265, Selected Issues Related to an Expansion of the Renewable Fuel Standard (RFS).)

Appliance and Lighting Efficiency Standards. Energy efficiency standards are set for broad categories of incandescent lamps (light bulbs), incandescent reflector lamps, and fluorescent lamps. A required target is set for lighting efficiency, and energy efficiency labeling is required for consumer electronic products. Also, efficiency standards are set by law for external power supplies, residential clothes washers, dishwashers, dehumidifiers, refrigerators, refrigerator-freezers, freezers, electric motors, residential boilers, commercial walk-in coolers, and commercial walk-in freezers. Further, DOE is directed to set standards by rulemaking for furnace fans and battery chargers.

Provisions Excluded

Two controversial provisions of H.R. 6 that were not included in the enacted law were the proposed Renewable Energy Portfolio Standard (RPS) and the proposed repeal of tax subsidies for oil and gas.

Renewable Energy Portfolio Standard (RPS). Under an RPS, retail electricity suppliers (electric utilities) must provide a minimum amount of electricity from renewable energy resources or purchase tradable credits that represent an equivalent amount of renewable energy production. The minimum requirement is often set as a percentage share of a supplier's total retail electricity sales. The second degree amendment to H.R. 6 passed by the House on December 6, 2007, proposed a national RPS target that aimed to reach 15% of total electricity sales by 2020. Up to 4 percentage points of the 15% target could be met with energy efficiency measures. This provision was stripped out by the Senate and was not included in the final version of the bill. (For more details on issues related to the RPS provision, see CRS Report RL34116, Renewable Energy Portfolio Standard (RPS): Background and Debate Over a National Requirement, by Fred Sissine.)

Energy Tax Subsidies. The House-passed second degree amendment to H.R. 6 contained provisions that would have repealed about $22 billion of oil and gas subsidies that were designed to offset the cost of supporting a variety of energy efficiency and renewable energy tax incentives. These proposed incentives would have included a four-year extension of the renewable energy electricity production tax credit. Most of those provisions were stripped out by the Senate and were not included in the final bill. Enough tax revenue offsets were included to cover the estimated cost of the CAFE provision. (For more details about the proposed renewable energy incentives, see CRS Report RL34162, Renewable Energy Issues in the 110th Congress, by Fred Sissine. For more details about the proposed repeal of oil and gas subsidies, see CRS Report RL33578, Energy Tax Policy, by Salvatore Lazzari.)

Brief Summary of Legislative Action

On January 18, 2007, the House passed the 14-page CLEAN Energy Act (H.R. 6) by a vote of 264-163. The bill proposed to repeal certain oil and natural gas subsidies, thus generating revenue for an Energy Efficiency and Renewables Reserve. The Reserve was designed to reduce foreign oil dependence and serve other purposes. The actual uses of the reserve would have been determined at a later date by further legislation. [1]

On June 21, 2007, the Senate passed its first degree amendments to H.R. 6 as the proposed Renewable Fuels, Consumer Protection, and Energy Efficiency Act of 2007. This action transformed H.R. 6 into a 500-page omnibus energy policy bill, with a primary focus on energy efficiency and renewable energy. The Senate's amendments were drawn primarily from the proposed Energy Savings Act of 2007 (S. 1321). [2] The key provisions of the Senate-passed H.R. 6 were appliance efficiency standards, an increase of the renewable fuel standard to 36 billion gallons by 2022, and an increase of the combined corporate average fuel economy standards to 35 miles per gallon (mpg) by 2020.

On August 4, 2007, the House passed the omnibus energy policy bill, H.R. 3221, which had two divisions and 13 titles. Division A contained provisions of the New Direction for

Energy Independence, National Security, and Consumer Protection Act. An adopted floor amendment (H.Amdt. 748) added a 15% renewable energy portfolio standard (RPS). Division B, the Renewable Energy and Energy Conservation Tax Act of 2007, was also added as a floor amendment and contained the House-approved version of H.R. 2776. It added four titles to H.R. 3221 that included a four-year extension of the renewable electricity production tax credit and other efficiency and renewables incentives.

Because the House omnibus bill (H.R. 3221) and the Senate omnibus bill (H.R. 6) had different bill numbers, the bills could not be taken directly to conference committee. [3] However, after the House completed action on H.R. 3221, informal bipartisan negotiations over the omnibus energy bills began between the House and Senate. Key issues included CAFE, the renewable fuel standard, the RPS provision in H.R. 3221, and a proposed repeal of certain oil and natural gas subsidies to offset costs for new energy efficiency and renewable energy tax incentives.

On December 6, 2007, the House passed by a vote of 235-181 its second-degree amendments to the Senate-passed amendments to H.R. 6. This "second version" of a House omnibus energy bill was derived primarily by trimming and modifying H.R. 3221 and adding major new provisions on CAFE and RFS. The House-passed bill included a proposed increase of the CAFE standard to 35 miles per gallon by 2020 and an increase of the renewable fuel standard to 36 billion gallons per year by 2022. The House bill also included a proposed 15% renewable electricity portfolio standard and $21 billion of new tax incentives for energy efficiency and renewable energy measures. The bill proposed to offset the new tax incentives with a repeal of about $21 billion in tax subsidies for oil and natural gas.

The White House threatened to veto the House-passed bill mainly because of the presence of provisions for an RPS and for the repeal of oil and gas tax subsidies. [4] On December 7, 2007, a Senate cloture vote on the House-passed version of H.R. 6 — with provisions for an RPS and for the repeal of oil and gas subsidies — failed (52-43). After stripping out the RPS and modifying the tax package, a cloture vote on S.Amdt. 3841 failed (59-40).

On December 13, 2007, the Senate adopted S.Amdt. 3850, its second-degree substitute amendment to H.R. 6 by a vote of 86-8. The Senate substitute was nearly identical to the House-passed bill, except that the RPS provision and most tax provisions had been taken out. The House approved the Senate bill on December 18, 2007. The President signed the bill into law on December 19, 2007 (P.L. 110-140).

TITLE I: ENERGY SECURITY THROUGH IMPROVED VEHICLE FUEL ECONOMY

Subtitle A, Increased Corporate Average Fuel Economy

This subtitle requires an increase in CAFE standards and a restructuring of the fuel economy program. A single CAFE standard of 35 miles per gallon (mpg) by MY2020 is established, and the distinction between the passenger car and light truck fleet is preserved. The new standards will be based on vehicle attributes and expressed in the form of a mathematical function. Interim standards will be set, beginning with MY2011. Manufacturers will be required to come within 92% of the standard for a given model year. However, manufacturers can earn credits for exceeding the standards in one vehicle class that can be applied to boost, within limitations, the CAFE of a different vehicle class that is falling short of compliance. Additionally, credits may be sold and bought between manufacturers. CAFE credits for the manufacture of flexible-fueled vehicles (FFV) are retained but phased out by MY2020. Civil penalties assessed for non-compliance will be deposited to the general fund of the U.S. Treasury to support future rulemaking and to provide grants to manufacturers for research and development, and retooling in support of increasing the fuel efficiency of their fleets. The law requires the development of standards for "work trucks" and commercial medium- and heavy-duty on-highway vehicles. (For additional information, see CRS Report RL33413, Automobile and Light Truck Fuel Economy: The CAFE Standards, by Brent D. Yacobucci and Robert Bamberger.)

Subtitle B, Improved Vehicle Technology

This subtitle establishes a loan guarantee program for advanced battery development, grant programs for plug-in hybrid vehicles, incentives for purchasing heavy-duty hybrid vehicles for fleets, and credits for various electric vehicles.

Subtitle C, Federal Vehicle Fleets

Federal agencies are prohibited from acquiring any light-duty motor vehicle or medium-duty passenger vehicle that is not "a low greenhouse gas emitting vehicle" as defined in this subtitle. Alternatively, the agency may demonstrate that it has adopted cost-effective policies to reduce its petroleum consumption sufficiently to achieve a comparable reduction in greenhouse gas emissions. By 2015, federal agencies are required to achieve at least a 20% reduction in annual petroleum consumption and a 10% increase in annual alternative fuel consumption. These increases are to be calculated from a 2005 baseline. Interim milestones will be established and agencies will report annually on their progress. The regulations governing this program are required to be issued not later than 18 months after enactment.

TITLE II: ENERGY SECURITY THROUGH INCREASED PRODUCTION OF BIOFUELS

Subtitle A, Renewable Fuel Standard

This subtitle extends and increases the renewable fuel standard (RFS) set by P.L. 109-58 (§1501). The RFS requires minimum annual levels of renewable fuel in U.S. transportation fuel. The previous standard was 5.4 billion gallons for 2008, rising to 7.5 billion by 2012. The new standard starts at 9.0 billion gallons in 2008 and rises to 36 billion gallons in 2022. Starting in 2016, all of the increase in the RFS target must be met with advanced biofuels, defined as cellulosic ethanol and other biofuels derived from feedstock other than corn starch

— with explicit carve-outs for cellulosic biofuels and biomass-based diesel. The EPA Administrator is given authority to temporarily waive part of the biofuels mandate, if it were determined that a significant renewable feedstock disruption or other market circumstance might occur. Renewable fuels produced from new biorefineries will be required to reduce by at least 20% the life cycle greenhouse gas (GHG) emissions relative to life cycle emissions from gasoline and diesel. Fuels produced from biorefineries that displace more than 80% of the fossil-derived processing fuels used to operate a biofuel production facility will qualify for cash awards. Several studies are required on the impacts of an RFS expansion on various sectors of the economy. (For more details on issues related to the RFS proposal, see CRS Report RL34265, Selected Issues Related to an Expansion of the Renewable Fuel Standard (RFS), by Brent D. Yacobucci and Randy Schnepf.)

Subtitle B, Biofuels Research and Development (R&D)

This subtitle promotes research on the expansion of the use of biodiesel and biogas as motor fuels. Grants are authorized for R&D and commercial applications of cellulosic biofuels technologies and for the conversion of existing corn-based ethanol plants to produce cellulosic biofuels. The Secretary of Energy is required to report to Congress on the feasibility of algae as a feedstock for biofuels production. The subtitle also promotes university-based R&D on biofuels.

Subtitle C, Biofuels Infrastructure

This subtitle aims to improve information about federal biofuels research programs, focus research on infrastructure and biorefineries, study potential impacts of increased biofuels use, and increase authorized funding for DOE biofuels research. A funding authorization of $25 million is established to provide grants for biofuels research, development, and demonstration (RD&D) and commercial applications in states that have low rates of ethanol production. A university-based program is authorized to provide grants of up to $2 million for R&D on renewable energy technologies. Priority is given to universities in low-income and rural communities with proximity to trees dying of disease or insect infestation.

DOE is directed to create a grant program to help establish or convert infrastructure to use renewable fuels, including E85 (85% ethanol). The Energy Policy Act of 2005 (EPACT, P.L. 109-58) authorization for grants to support cellulosic ethanol production is increased. A grant program is authorized to support production of flexible-fueled vehicles. Studies are also required on the market penetration of flexible-fueled vehicles, the feasibility of constructing dedicated ethanol pipelines, the feasibility of using greater percentages of ethanol in fuel blends, and the adequacy of railroad transportation for delivery of ethanol fuel.

Subtitle D, Environmental Safeguards

Previously, under the Clean Air Act (§211[f]), no new fuels or fuel additives could be introduced into commerce unless granted a waiver by the Environmental Protection Agency

(EPA). If EPA did not act within 180 days of receiving a waiver request, the waiver was treated as granted. [5] Section 251 tightens the waiver provision. It amends the Clean Air Act to prohibit the introduction of new fuels or fuel additives unless EPA explicitly grants a waiver. After receiving a waiver request, EPA will now have 270 days to take final action.

TITLE III: ENERGY SAVINGS THROUGH IMPROVED STANDARDS FOR APPLIANCES AND LIGHTING

Subtitle A, Appliance Energy Efficiency

This title sets, by statute, new efficiency standards for external power supplies, residential clothes washers, dishwashers, dehumidifiers, refrigerators, refrigerator-freezers, freezers, electric motors, and residential boilers. DOE is allowed to establish regional variations in standards for heating and air conditioning equipment. DOE is required to complete a rulemaking process for furnace fans by 2013. Federal agencies are directed to purchase devices that limit standby power use. DOE is directed to issue a final rule that sets efficiency standards for battery chargers. Certain energy efficiency measures for walk-in coolers and walk-in freezers are set by law. Also, several procedural changes are now in place to expedite the DOE rulemaking process.

Subtitle B, Lighting Energy Efficiency

Section 321 sets an energy efficiency standard for general service incandescent lamps, provides for consumer education and lamp labeling, and requires market assessments and a consumer awareness program. Section 322 sets energy efficiency standards for incandescent reflector lamps and fluorescent lamps. For federal buildings, Section 323 sets energy efficiency requirements for GSA-leased space and for use of energy efficient lighting fixtures and bulbs in those leased spaces. Section 324 sets energy efficiency standards for metal halide lamp fixtures designed to be operated with lamps rated between 150 watts and 500 watts. Section 325 directs the Consumer Product Safety Commission to set energy efficiency labeling requirements for consumer electronic products.

TITLE IV: ENERGY SAVINGS IN BUILDINGS AND INDUSTRY

Subtitle A, Residential Building Efficiency

Section 411 increases the funding authorization for DOE's Weatherization Program, providing $3.75 billion over five years. Under Section 412, DOE is directed to conduct a study of the renewable energy system rebate program described in §206(c) of the Energy Policy Act of 2005. The study aims to determine the minimum funding the program would need to be viable. Further, DOE is directed to propose an implementation plan. Section 413 requires DOE to establish energy efficiency standards for manufactured housing.

Subtitle B, High-Performance Commercial Buildings

This subtitle encourages the development of more energy-efficient "green" commercial buildings. Section 421 creates an Office of Commercial High Performance Green Buildings at DOE. Section 422 establishes a zero-energy commercial buildings initiative. A national goal is set to achieve zero-net-energy use for new commercial buildings built after 2025. A further goal is to retrofit all pre2025 buildings to zero-net-energy use by 2050. Section 423 requires that DOE establish a national clearinghouse for information and public outreach about high-performance green buildings.

Subtitle C, High-Performance Federal Buildings

Section 431 requires that total energy use in federal buildings, relative to the 2005 level, be reduced 30% by 2015. Section 432 directs that federal energy managers conduct a comprehensive energy and water evaluation for each facility at least once every four years. For new federal buildings and major renovations, Section 433 requires that fossil-fuel energy use — relative to the 2003 level — be reduced 55% by 2010 and be eliminated (100% reduction) by 2030. Section 434 requires that each federal agency ensure that major replacements of installed equipment (such as heating and cooling systems), or renovation or expansion of existing space, employ the most energy efficient designs, systems, equipment, and controls that are life-cycle cost effective. Section 435 prohibits federal agencies from leasing buildings that have not earned an EPA Energy Star label. Section 436 requires GSA to establish an Office of Federal High-Performance Green Buildings to coordinate green building information and activities within GSA and with other federal agencies. The Office must also develop standards for federal facilities, establish green practices, review budget and life-cycle costing issues, and promote demonstration of innovative technologies. Section 437 directs the Government Accountability Office (GAO) to audit the implementation of activities required under this subtitle. The audit must cover budget, life-cycle costing, contracting, best practices, and agency coordination. Section 438 requires federal facility development projects with a footprint exceeding 5,000 square feet to use site planning, design, construction, and maintenance strategies to control storm water runoff. Section 439 directs GSA to review the current use of, and design a strategy for increased use of, cost-effective lighting, ground source heat pumps, and other technologies in GSA facilities. Section 440 authorizes $4 million per year over five years to support work under sections 434-439 and 482. For the purpose of conducting life-cycle cost calculations, Section 441 increases the time period from 25 years, in prior law, to 40 years.

Subtitle D, Industrial Energy Efficiency

Section 451 directs DOE to conduct research on, develop, and demonstrate new processes, technologies, and operating practices and techniques to significantly improve the energy efficiency of equipment and processes used by energy-intensive industries. Section 452 directs EPA to establish a recoverable waste energy inventory program. This program must include an ongoing survey of all major industrial and large commercial combustion sources in the United States. EPA is required to identify the potential for economically feasible waste energy recovery, create a grant program to support waste energy recovery, and strengthen "clean energy centers" that analyze waste energy recovery. Section 453 directs DOE to initiate a voluntary national information program for widely used data centers and data center equipment for which there is significant potential for energy savings. DOE is also tasked with helping to devise strategies to improve energy efficiency at these data centers.

Subtitle E, Healthy High-Performance Schools

Section 461 creates a grant program for Healthy High-Performance Schools that aims to encourage states, local governments, and school systems to build green schools. EPA, in consultation with the Department of Education, is allowed to provide grants to state agencies to provide technical assistance and help with the development of state plans for school building design. Also, EPA is directed to develop model voluntary guidelines for school site selection. In addition to other environmental aspects, the grants and guidelines must have a focus on energy efficiency, natural daylighting, and other energy-related features. Section 462 directs EPA to lead a detailed study of how sustainable building features, such as energy efficiency, affect multiple perceived indoor environmental quality stressors on students in K-12 schools.

Subtitle F, Institutional Entities

Section 471 creates a program of grants and loans to support energy efficiency and energy sustainability projects at public institutions.

Subtitle G, Public and Assisted Housing

Section 481 directs the Department of Housing and Urban Development (HUD) to update energy efficiency standards for all public and assisted housing.

Subtitle H, General Provisions

Section 491 calls for the DOE Office of Commercial High Performance Buildings and the GSA Office of Federal High Performance Buildings to jointly develop guidelines for demonstration projects. In accordance with the guidelines, one federal project must be undertaken annually over a five-year period, supported by a $10 million funding authorization. Also, a total of four projects are to be undertaken at different universities over the five-year period, supported by an additional $10 million funding authorization. Section 492 calls for these two offices to undertake a joint survey of research on green buildings, coordinate efforts to develop a research plan, and identify potential benefits of green buildings for security, natural disasters, and emergency needs of the federal government.

Section 493 requires EPA to create a program of competitive grants to local governments for green building demonstration projects. Section 494 directs the Office of Commercial High Performance Buildings and the Office of Federal High Performance Buildings to jointly appoint a Green Building Advisory Committee with representatives from a variety of backgrounds, including federal agencies, state and local governments, building industry experts, security advisors, and environmental health experts. Section 495 calls for DOE to create an advisory committee on energy efficiency finance to help lower costs and increase investment for energy efficiency technologies.

TITLE V: ENERGY SAVINGS IN GOVERNMENT AND PUBLIC INSTITUTIONS

Subtitle A, United States Capitol Complex

Section 501 allows the Architect of the Capitol (AOC) to perform a feasibility study regarding construction of a photovoltaic roof for the Rayburn House Office Building. Under Section 502, the AOC is allowed to construct a fuel tank and pumping system for E85 (85% ethanol) fuel at or within close proximity to the Capitol Grounds Fuel Station. Section 503 requires the AOC, to the maximum extent practicable, to include energy efficiency measures, climate change mitigation measures, and other appropriate environmental measures in the Capitol Complex Master Plan. Under Section 504, the AOC is directed to operate the steam boilers and chiller plant at the Capitol Power Plant in the most energy efficient manner possible to minimize carbon emissions and operating costs. Further, Section 505 requires the AOC to install technologies for the capture and storage or use of carbon dioxide emitted from coal combustion in the Capitol Power Plant.

Subtitle B, Energy Savings Performance Contracting

Section 511 eliminates the advance reporting requirement for Energy Savings Performance Contracts (ESPCs) that have a cancellation ceiling exceeding $10 million. Section 512 increases ESPC funding flexibility by allowing a combination of appropriated funds and private financing. Section 513 restricts federal agencies from limiting the duration of ESPCs to less than 25 years or limiting the total amount of obligations. Further, this section permits the criteria for savings verification to satisfy the requirement for energy audits. Also, it directs federal agencies to modify existing ESPCs to conform with the requirements of this subtitle. Section 514 permanently authorizes ESPCs.

Section 515 extends the definition of energy savings reduction to include increased use of an existing energy source by cogeneration or heat recovery, use of excess electrical or thermal energy generated from onsite renewable sources or cogeneration, and increased energy-efficient use of water resources. Section 516 permits agencies to retain the full amount of energy and water cost savings obtained from utility incentive programs. Section 517 authorizes $750,000 per year over five years for a program to train contract officers in negotiating ESPCs. Section 518 directs the Department of Defense (DOD) and DOE to study the potential use of ESPCs in nonbuilding applications, which is defined to include vehicles and federally owned equipment to generate electricity or transport water.

Subtitle C, Energy Efficiency in Federal Agencies

Under Section 521, GSA is directed to use up to $30 million — subject to appropriation — from FY2007 and prior years' unobligated balances of the Federal Buildings Fund to support the installation of a solar photovoltaic system for the DOE headquarters building in the District of Columbia. Section 522 prohibits, except under certain circumstances, the purchase of incandescent light bulbs for use in Coast Guard office buildings. Section 523 requires 30% of the hot water demand in new federal buildings (and major renovations) to be met with solar hot water equipment, provided it is life-cycle cost-effective. Section 524 encourages federal agencies to minimize standby energy use in purchases of energy-using equipment. Section 525 requires federal procurement to focus on use of Energy Star and Federal Energy Management Program (FEMP)-designated products. Section 526 prohibits federal agencies from procuring synfuel unless its life cycle GHG emissions are less than those for conventional petroleum sources. Section 527 directs each federal agency subject to any requirements under this title to issue an annual report that describes the status of initiatives to improve energy efficiency, reduce energy costs, and reduce GHG emissions. Section 528 requires the Office of Management and Budget (OMB) to submit an annual report to Congress that summarizes the information reported under Section 527, evaluates overall progress toward the goals of Section 527, and recommends additional actions needed to meet those goals. Section 529 directs the Federal Energy Regulatory Commission (FERC) to conduct a national assessment of demand response, including an estimate of nationwide demand response out to a 10year horizon. Further, FERC is required to prepare a National Action Plan on Demand Response, with cooperation from industry. Annual funding of $10 million per year is authorized over three years.

Subtitle D, Energy Efficiency of Public Institutions

Section 531 increases annual funding authorizations for DOE's state energy programs. Under Section 532, electric and natural gas utilities are required to make energy efficiency a priority resource and to integrate energy efficiency into resource plans and planning processes. Further, the utilities are directed to modify their rates to align their incentives with the delivery of cost-effective energy efficiency and promote energy efficiency investments. Utilities are encouraged to consider several policy options for achieving those goals.

Subtitle E, Energy Efficiency and Conservation Block Grants

This subtitle establishes an energy efficiency block grant program. Section 541 provides definitions of program elements. Section 542 directs DOE to establish an energy efficiency and conservation block grant program to help reduce energy use and emissions at the local and regional level. Section 543 establishes allocation percentages for grants provided under this subtitle. Section 544 enumerates the allowed purposes for the use of funds provided under this subtitle, which includes strategic planning, consultant services, and energy audits. Section 545 provides eligibility requirements for grants under this program, including payment of prevailing wage rates, submission of a strategic plan, and sharing of information. Section 546 sets criteria for minimum allocations of competitive grant funding. Section 547 specifies that DOE may review and evaluate the performance of grant recipients and withhold funds from those it deems have failed to achieve compliance. To support the grant program, Section 548 authorizes $2 billion annually over five years. Additional funding is authorized to cover administrative costs of the program. Section 548 stresses that funding will supplement, not replace, funding provided by DOE under the Weatherization and State Energy programs.

TITLE VI: ACCELERATED RESEARCH AND DEVELOPMENT

Subtitle A, Solar Energy

Section 602 aims to improve the cost and effectiveness of thermal energy storage technologies that could improve the operation of concentrating solar power electric generating plants. Section 603 calls for improved integration of concentrating solar power into regional electricity transmission systems.

Subtitle B, Geothermal Energy

DOE is directed to support programs of R&D, demonstration, and commercial application to expand the use of geothermal energy. Section 613 directs DOE to support programs that (1) develop advanced prospecting tools to locate and develop hidden geothermal resources, and (2) demonstrate advanced exploratory drilling technologies and techniques with industry partners. Section 614 directs DOE to support programs to develop components and systems necessary to develop, produce, monitor, and model the performance of geothermal reservoirs used to produce geothermal energy. In addition, Section 614 directs DOE to support programs that mitigate or prevent environmental damage from geothermal energy development.

Section 615 directs DOE to support enhanced geothermal system development, whereby geothermal reservoir systems are engineered (as opposed to naturally occurring systems) by creating fractures and permeable conduits via reservoir stimulation. DOE would support R&D programs for enhanced geothermal system technologies and for reservoir stimulation and support demonstration projects at a minimum of four sites.

DOE is directed to establish a program of R&D, demonstration, and commercial application for geothermal energy production from oil and gas fields and from geopressured resources.6 Section 616 directs DOE to implement a grant program for at least three demonstration projects that use geothermal techniques to extract energy from marginal, unproductive, and productive oil and gas fields. Also, DOE is directed to establish a grant program for the recovery of energy from geopressured resources.

Section 618 directs DOE to establish a Center for Geothermal Technology Transfer, via a grant to an institution of higher learning or consortium thereof, that would serve as an information clearinghouse for the geothermal industry, make data available to the public, and coordinate R&D efforts among national and international partners. Section 619 would rename DOE's GeoPowering the West program as "GeoPowering America" and expand its geothermal technology transfer activities to cover the entire United States. Section 620 would award a grant on a competitive basis to an institution of higher education to establish a geothermal-powered energy generation facility on the institution's campus.

Section 624 directs DOE to support international geothermal energy development through collaborative efforts to promote geothermal R&D and deployment of geothermal technologies. Section 625 directs DOE to make grants to eligible entities from "high-cost regions" [7] of the United States for a feasibility study, demonstration, and commercial application of technologies related to geothermal energy.

Subtitle B authorizes $90 million annually for geothermal activities, of which $10 million is designated for activities under Section 616. An additional $5 million is authorized annually for the Intermountain West Geothermal Consortium, and $5 million is authorized annually for Section 624. All of the foregoing authorizations are in effect from 2008 to 2012.

Subtitle C, Marine and Hydrokinetic Renewable Energy Technologies

DOE is directed to create an R&D program focused on technology that produces electricity from waves, tides, currents, and ocean thermal differences (§633). A report to Congress is required. Further, DOE is instructed to award grants to institutions of higher education (or consortia thereof) to establish National Marine Renewable Energy Research, Development, and Demonstration Centers (§634).

Subtitle D, Energy Storage for Transportation and Electric Power

The U.S. Energy Storage Competitiveness Act of 2007 directs DOE to conduct a cost-shared RD&D program to support the ability of the nation to remain globally competitive in energy storage systems for electric drive vehicles, stationary applications, and electricity transmission and distribution. An Energy Storage Advisory Council will be created, with responsibility for preparing a five-year research plan. Also, through competitive bids, DOE will establish four energy storage research centers managed by the Office of Science. DOE is required to conduct energy storage demonstration projects. Also, DOE is to investigate secondary applications of energy storage equipment and to examine technologies and processes for final recycling and disposal of energy storage equipment. After five years of program operation, the law will require a review of the program by the National Academy of Sciences. A total authorization of nearly $3 billion is provided over a 10-year period.

Subtitle E, Miscellaneous Provisions

Section 651 directs DOE to establish an RD&D program to determine ways in which the weight of motor vehicles could be reduced to improve fuel efficiency without compromising passenger safety. This will focus on the development of new materials and on reducing the cost of lightweight materials. An $80 million authorization is provided over a five-year period.

Section 652 directs DOE to report on the state of technology development for "advanced" insulation with an R-value greater than R35 per inch. The report is to include an estimate of potential cost savings by applying such insulation to covered refrigeration units. If sufficient cost savings are projected, DOE will then be directed to conduct a cost-shared demonstration program to show actual cost savings. An $8 million funding authorization is provided for that program.

Section 653 changes the sulfur dioxide (SO_2) criterion for clean coal power plants from a percentage basis (99% of SO_2 removed) to a weight-by-energy basis (no more than 0.04 pounds of SO_2 per million Btu).

Section 654 on the "H-Prize" directs DOE to conduct a competitive program to award cash prizes to advance R&D, demonstration, and commercial application of hydrogen energy technologies. Prizes can be a mix of federal appropriations and funds provided by an entity that DOE chooses to administer the program. The program sunsets in 2018. Prize categories include technology advancements in hydrogen production, storage, distribution, and use; prototypes of hydrogen vehicles and products; and technologies that "transform" distribution or production. DOE is required to report to Congress annually, identifying award recipients, technologies developed, and specific actions undertaken to commercialize the technologies. More than $1 billion is authorized over a 10-year period.

Section 655 directs DOE to create the "Bright Tomorrow" lighting prizes for solid state (LED) lighting developments that achieve targeted levels of energy efficiency and other traits. Two specific categories are a solid state replacement for a 60-watt incandescent light and a replacement for the PAR Type 38 halogen light. Also, a prize is established for a "twenty-first century lamp" that achieves certain output, efficiency, and color targets. After the awards are made, DOE is required to develop guidelines for federal agency purchases of the incandescent and halogen replacements, with the goal of complete replacement within five years.

Section 656 directs DOE to establish a cost-shared Renewable Energy Innovation Manufacturing Partnership Program to make awards to support RD&D on advanced manufacturing processes, materials, and infrastructure for renewable energy technologies. Further goals are to increase domestic renewable energy production and better coordinate federal, state, and private resources through partnerships. Solar, wind, biomass, geothermal, energy storage, and fuel cell systems are eligible forms of equipment.

TITLE VII: CARBON CAPTURE AND SEQUESTRATION

Subtitle A, Carbon Capture and Sequestration Research, Development, and Demonstration

DOE's program for carbon capture and sequestration R&D is expanded and will include large-scale demonstration projects. DOE is directed to engage the National Academy of Sciences (NAS) to conduct a review of the program. DOE is directed to work with the NAS to develop interdisciplinary graduate degree programs with emphasis on geologic sequestration science. A university-based R&D grant program will be established to study carbon capture and sequestration using various types of coal. EPA is directed to assess potential impacts of carbon sequestration on public health and safety and the environment. Further, injection and sequestration activities under this subtitle are subject to the requirements of the Safe Drinking Water Act.

Subtitle B, Carbon Capture and Sequestration Assessment and Framework

Section 711 directs the Department of the Interior (DOI) to develop a methodology for an assessment of the national potential for geologic storage of carbon dioxide. Following publication of the methodology, DOI will be required to complete an assessment of national capacity for carbon dioxide storage in accordance with the methodology.

Section 712 directs DOI to develop a methodology for an assessment of the total capacity of ecosystems to sequester carbon and the ability of ecosystems to reduce emissions of carbon dioxide, methane, and nitrous oxides in ecosystems through management practices. Following publication of the methodology, DOI will be required to complete a national assessment of the quantity of carbon stored in and released from ecosystems, and the annual flux of carbon dioxide, methane, and nitrous oxides in and out of ecosystems.

Section 713 calls for DOI to maintain records, and an inventory, of the quantity of carbon dioxide stored within federal mineral leaseholds.

Section 714 directs DOI to submit a report on a recommended regulatory framework for managing geologic carbon sequestration on public lands. The report must include an assessment of options to ensure that the United States receives fair market value for the use of public land, the proposed procedures for public review and comment, procedures for protecting natural and cultural resources of the public land overlying the geologic sequestration sites, a description of the status of liability issues related to the storage of carbon dioxide in public land, identification of legal and regulatory issues for cases where the United States owns title to the mineral resources but not the overlying land, identification of issues related to carbon dioxide pipeline rights-of-way, and recommendations for additional legislation that may be required for adequate public land management and leasing to accommodate geologic sequestration of carbon dioxide and pipeline rights-of-way.

TITLE VIII: IMPROVED MANAGEMENT OF ENERGY POLICY

Subtitle A, Management Improvements

Section 801 directs DOE to conduct a 10-year national media campaign to educate consumers to save energy and reduce oil use. Competitive bidding is required for contracting the media services. A funding authorization of $5 million per year is provided for five years. An annual report to Congress is required.

Section 802 authorizes the Federal Coordinator for the Alaska Natural Gas Transportation Projects to appoint and terminate personnel and to pay appointed and temporary personnel up to a maximum of the level III rate of the Executive Schedule. The Federal Coordinator is granted authority to establish various payment requirements and to use funds raised without further appropriation. This authority does not affect the authority of the Secretary of the Interior.

Section 803 creates a 50% matching grant program for constructing small renewable energy projects that will have an electrical generation capacity less than 15 megawatts. Eligible applicants include local governments, utilities, and Indian tribes. Such sums as necessary are authorized for the program.

Section 804 requires the Energy Information Administration (EIA) to monitor planned petroleum refinery outages and report to the Secretary of Energy when such outages are affecting the price or availability of petroleum products. The Secretary will then be required to share data with refinery operators and encourage reductions in out-of-service refinery capacity.

Section 805 requires the Administrator of the Energy Information Administration (EIA) to develop a five-year plan for enhancing the scope, quality, and timeliness of the agency's data collection efforts. In addition, it requires closer coordination by EIA with state energy officials and with the Federal Energy Regulatory Commission. The section addresses state-level data in several respects and requires the Administrator to submit to Congress within a year an assessment of state level energy data needs. EIA is directed to revisit certain data series that had been terminated due to budget constraints and to identify data gaps that may have resulted from those terminations. To implement this section, $10 million is authorized for 2008, and additional sums are authorized through 2012.

Section 806 expresses the sense of Congress that there is a national goal to use renewable energy resources from agricultural, forestry, and working lands of the nation to provide at least 25% of the nation's energy use by 2025.

Section 807 directs the Department of the Interior's U.S. Geological Survey to conduct a comprehensive assessment of geothermal energy resources in the United States and report the findings of that assessment to Congress.

Subtitle B, Prohibitions on Market Manipulation and False Information

This subtitle prohibits crude oil and petroleum product wholesalers from using any technique to manipulate the market or provide false information. The law directs the Federal

Trade Commission to treat such action as an unfair or deceptive practice, subject to civil penalties of not more than $1 million per incident.

Title IX: International Energy Programs

This title authorizes assistance to promote clean and efficient energy technologies in foreign countries, and it establishes an International Clean Energy Foundation.

Subtitle A, Assistance to Promote Clean and Efficient Energy Technologies in Foreign Countries

The U.S. Agency for International Development (USAID) is directed to report to Congress on efforts to support policies for clean and efficient energy technologies. The Department of Commerce is directed to increase efforts to export such technologies and report to Congress on the results. Other U.S. agencies with export promotion responsibilities are required to increase efforts to support these technologies. Also, a multi-agency Task Force on International Cooperation for Clean and Efficient Energy Technologies is created to support the implementation of clean energy markets in key developing countries.

Section 917 creates a U.S.-Israel Energy Cooperation partnership to support research, development, and deployment (RD&D) of energy efficiency and renewable energy measures.

Subtitle B, International Clean Energy Foundation

The Foundation is established with the long-term goal of reducing GHG emissions. It is directed to use the funds authorized by this subtitle to make grants to promote projects outside of the United States that serve as models of how to reduce emissions. An annual report to Congress is required.

Subtitle C, Miscellaneous Provisions

Section 931 calls for the Secretary of State to ensure that energy security is integrated into the core mission of the Department of State. Energy advisors are required at key embassies, and the Department is required to report to Congress every two years on its energy-related activities. Section 932 adds the Secretary of Energy to the National Security Council. Section 933 calls for the President to submit to Congress a comprehensive annual report that describes a national energy security strategy for the nation.

Section 934 implements the Convention on Supplementary Compensation for Nuclear Damage that was opened for signature in 1997. The convention has since been signed by the United States and 12 other countries but has not yet entered into force. Each party to the convention will be required to establish a compensation system within its borders for nuclear damages to the public. In the United States, this obligation will be fulfilled by the existing

Price-Anderson Act (§170 of the Atomic Energy Act of 1954). The convention will also establish a second tier of damage compensation to be paid by all parties. Section 934 requires the U.S. contribution to the second tier to be paid by suppliers of nuclear equipment and services, under a formula to be developed by DOE. Supporters of the convention contend that it will help U.S. exporters of nuclear technology by establishing a predictable international liability system.

Section 935 has the stated purpose of improving national energy security by promoting anti-corruption initiatives in oil and natural gas rich countries and of improving global energy security by promoting programs such as the Extractive Industries Transparency Initiative (EITI) that aim to increase transparency and accountability into extractive resource payments. The sense of Congress is expressed that global energy security should be furthered by encouraging further participation in EITI by eligible countries and companies and by promoting the effectiveness of the EITI program by ensuring that a robust and candid review mechanism is put in place. The Secretary of State is required to report to Congress on progress made in promoting transparency in extractive industries resource payments. An authorization of $3 million is provided to support U.S. contributions to the Multi-Donor Trust Fund of EITI.

TITLE X: GREEN JOBS

This title authorizes up to $125 million in funding to establish national and state job training programs, administered by the Department of Labor, to help address job shortages that are impairing growth in green industries, such as energy efficient buildings and construction, renewable electric power, energy efficient vehicles, and biofuels development.

TITLE XI: ENERGY TRANSPORTATION AND INFRASTRUCTURE

Subtitle A, Department of Transportation (DOT)

An Office of Climate Change and Environment is established at DOT to plan, coordinate, and implement strategies to reduce transportation-related energy use, mitigate the effects of climate change, and address the impact of climate change on transportation systems and infrastructure.

Subtitle B, Railroads

This subtitle directs DOT, in coordination with EPA, to establish and conduct a pilot grant program to assist railroad carriers in purchasing hybrid locomotives, including hybrid switch locomotives, in order to demonstrate the extent to which such locomotives increase fuel economy, reduce emissions, and lower costs of operation. Also, DOT is directed to create a program of capital grants for the rehabilitation, preservation, or improvement of railroad track (including roadbed, bridges, and related track structures) of class II and class III railroads.

Subtitle C, Marine Transportation

Short sea transportation is defined as commercial waterborne transportation that originates at a port in the United States and ends at another port in the United States or at a port in Canada located in the Great Lakes Saint Lawrence Seaway System. The same definition applies for the case where origination and end points are reversed. [8] This subtitle directs DOT to establish a short sea transportation program and designate short sea transportation projects to be conducted under the program to mitigate landside congestion. Short sea shipping activities are made eligible for support from DOT's capital construction fund. A report to Congress on the short sea transportation program is required.

Subtitle D, Highways

Section 1131 increases the federal share for congestion mitigation and air quality (CMAQ) projects up to 100% of project or program cost. Under Section 1132, DOT is directed to redistribute within each state any unobligated balances of the Highway Trust Fund that are rescinded in FY2008 or FY2009. Section 1133 expresses a sense of Congress that, in constructing new roadways or rehabilitating existing facilities, state and local governments should employ policies designed to accommodate all users, including motorists, pedestrians, cyclists, transit riders, and people of all ages and abilities.

TITLE XII: SMALL BUSINESS ENERGY PROGRAMS

Loans, grants, and debentures are established to help small businesses develop, invest in, and purchase energy efficient buildings, fixtures, equipment, and technology. Section 1201 empowers the Small Business Administration (SBA) to make "express" loans for certain energy efficiency and renewable energy projects. Section 1202 creates a two-year pilot loan program for purchasing energy efficient technologies under Section 7(a) of the Small Business Act at half the cost that would have otherwise been required. After the pilot program terminates, GAO is required to prepare a report to Congress that describes its energy-saving impact. Section 1203 creates small business energy efficiency, sustainability, and telecommuting programs. Reports to Congress are required for each of those programs. Section 1204 raises the Small Business Investment Act (SBIA) loan ceilings for certain energy efficiency and renewable energy projects undertaken by small businesses. Section 1205 enables qualified small business investment companies to issue energy-saving debentures.

Section 1206 expands certain SBIA provisions to include investments in energy-saving small businesses. Section 1207 creates a Renewable Fuel Capital Investment (RFCI) pilot program that taps into venture capital to help small firms develop renewable energy sources and new technologies. A funding authorization of $30 million is provided for RFCI over two years. Section 1208 requires SBA to study the RFCI program and issue a report to Congress on its findings.

TITLE XIII: SMART GRID

Section 1301 establishes a federal policy to modernize the electric utility transmission and distribution system to maintain reliability and infrastructure protection. The term "Smart Grid" refers to a distribution system that allows for flow of information from a customer's meter in two directions: both inside the house to thermostats, appliances, and other devices, and from the house back to the utility.9 Smart Grid is defined to include a variety of operational and energy measures — including smart meters, smart appliances, renewable energy resources, and energy efficiency resources. Section 1302 calls for DOE to report to Congress on the deployment of Smart Grid technologies and any barriers to deployment. Section 1303 directs DOE to establish a Smart Grid Advisory Committee and a Smart Grid Task Force to assist with implementation. Section 1304 directs DOE to conduct Smart Grid RD&D and to develop measurement strategies to assess energy savings and other aspects of implementation. Section 1305 directs the National Institute of Standards and Technology to establish protocols and standards to increase the flexibility of use for Smart Grid equipment and systems. Section 1306 directs DOE to create a program that reimburses 20% of qualifying Smart Grid investments. Section 1307 directs states to encourage utilities to employ Smart Grid technology and allows utilities to recover Smart Grid investments through rates. Section 1308 requires DOE to prepare a report to Congress on the effect of private wire laws on the development of combined heat and power facilities. Section 1309 directs DOE to report to Congress on the potential impacts of Smart Grid deployment on the security of electricity infrastructure and operating capability. (For additional information, see CRS Report RL34288, Smart Grid Provisions in H.R. 6, 110th Congress, by Amy Abel.)

TITLE XIV: POOL AND SPA SAFETY

Section 1401 identifies this title as the "Virginia Graeme Baker Pool and Spa Safety Act." Section 1402 finds that proper use of barriers or fencing could substantially reduce the number of childhood residential swimming and pool drownings. Section 1403 provides several definitions employed throughout this subtitle. Section 1404 sets an industry standard (ASME/ANSI A112.19.8) as a national performance standard for swimming pool and spa drain cover equipment. Section 1405 establishes a grant program and requires that at least 50% of the funding be used to assist states in hiring and training enforcement personnel to implement and enforce standards. The remaining funds must be used to educate pool construction and installation companies, pool owners and operators, and pool service companies, about the standard. Also, funding of $2 million per year over two years is authorized for the federal Consumer Product Safety Commission to implement the grant program. Section 1406 specifies minimum state law requirements to qualify for a grant under Section 1405. The requirement includes the enclosure of all outdoor residential pools and spas, installation of devices to prevent entrapment by pool or spa drains, and notification to pool owners about entrapment protection standards. Also, in setting minimum state law requirements, the Commission is directed to consider current or revised national standards for barrier and entrapment equipment, and to ensure that the requirements are consistent with the Commission's existing publications on pool safety guidelines. Section 1407 directs the Commission to conduct a public education program on methods to prevent drowning and entrapment in swimming pools. A funding authorization of $5 million per year is provided over five years. Section 1408 directs the Commission to submit a report to Congress that evaluates the implementation of the state grant program.

TITLE XV: REVENUE PROVISIONS

Section 1500 specifies that, unless expressed otherwise, all tax provisions in this act refer to provisions of the Internal Revenue Code of 1986.

Section 1501 extends Federal Unemployment Tax Act (FUTA) taxes for one year. FUTA imposes a 6.2% gross tax rate on the first $7,000 paid annually by covered employers to each employee. In 1976, Congress passed a temporary surtax of 0.2% of taxable wages to be added to the permanent FUTA tax rate. The temporary surtax was subsequently extended through 2007. The President's FY2008 Budget had proposed extending the FUTA surtax. The Treasury Department stated that "extending the surtax will support the continued solvency of the federal unemployment trust funds and maintain the ability of the unemployment system to adjust to any economic downturns." This section enacts the President's proposal for one year, 2008. This provision is estimated to raise $1.446 billion over 10 calendar years.

Under Section 1502, the geological and geophysical costs of a major integrated oil company will be amortized (deducted proportionally) over a seven-year period instead of the current five-year period. (A major integrated oil company is defined as one with an average world production of at least 500,000 barrels per day, with 2005 gross receipts exceeding $1 billion, and which has at least a 15% interest in refinery operations.)

TITLE XVI: EFFECTIVE DATE

Section 1601 specifies that this act and the amendments it makes will take effect one day after enactment.

REFERENCE

[1] For more details about the reserve, see CRS Report RS22571, The Strategic Energy Efficiency and Renewables Reserve in the CLEAN Energy Act of 2007 (H.R. 6, by Fred Sissine).

[2] S. 1321 was, in turn, derived from several other Senate bills. Additional details about legislation that was incorporated into H.R. 6 are available in CRS Report RL33831, Energy Efficiency and Renewable Energy Legislation in the 110th Congress, by Fred Sissine, Lynn J. Cunningham, and Mark Gurevitz.

[3] More details about the House and Senate bills developed up to that point are available in CRS Report RL34135, Omnibus Energy Efficiency and Renewable Energy Legislation: A Side-by-Side Comparison of Major Provisions in House-Passed H.R. 3221 with Senate-Passed H.R. 6, by Fred Sissine.

[4] Office of Management and Budget, Statement of Administration Policy on H.R. 6, Energy Independence and Security Act of 2007, December 6, 2007; [http://www.whitehouse.gov/ omb/legislative/sap/110-1/hr6sap-h_2.pdf].

[5] See 42 U.S.C. 7545(f).

[6] Geopressured resources are geothermal deposits of hot water or steam found in sedimentary rocks under higher than normal pressures and that are saturated with oil andgas.

[7] These "high cost" regions are defined as places where the average cost of retail power exceeds 150% of the national average.

[8] This is the definition offered in Section 1122. Also, see the definition provided in Short Sea Shipping: Practices, Opportunities, and Challenges, by Gary A. Lombardo, [http://www.insourceaudit.com/WhitePapers/Short_Sea_Shipping.asp].

[9] The Smart Grid could allow appliances to be turned off during periods of high electrical demand and cost and give customers real-time information on constantly changing electric rates. The goal is to use advanced, information-based technologies to increase power grid efficiency, reliability, and flexibility, and reduce the rate at which additional electric utility infrastructure needs to be built.

In: Energy Policy: Issues, Actions and Consequences
Editor: Quentin V. Harris
ISBN 978-1-60692-225-5

Chapter 4

BIOFUELS INCENTIVES: A SUMMARY OF FEDERAL PROGRAMS*

Brent D. Yacobucci

ABSTRACT

With recent high energy prices and the passage of major energy legislation in 2005 (P.L. 109-58) and 2007 (P.L. 110-140), there is ongoing congressional interest in promoting alternatives to petroleum fuels. Biofuels — transportation fuels produced from plants and other organic materials — are of particular interest.

Ethanol and biodiesel, the two most widely used biofuels, receive significant government support under this law in the form of mandated fuel use, tax incentives, loan and grant programs, and certain regulatory requirements. The 18 programs and provisions listed in this report have been established over the past 27 years, and are administered by five separate agencies and departments: Environmental Protection Agency, U.S. Department of Agriculture, Department of Energy, Internal Revenue Service, and Customs and Border Protection. These programs target a variety of beneficiaries, including farmers and rural small businesses, biofuel producers, petroleum suppliers, and fuel marketers. Arguably, the most significant federal programs for biofuels have been tax credits for the production or sale of ethanol and biodiesel. However, with the establishment of the renewable fuels standard (RFS) under P.L. 109-58, Congress has mandated biofuels use; P.L. 110-140 significantly expanded that mandate. In the long term, the mandate may prove even more significant than tax incentives in promoting the use of these fuels.

This report outlines federal programs that provide direct or indirect incentives for biofuels. For each program described, the report provides details including administering agency, authorizing statute(s), annual funding, and expiration date. The Appendix provides summary information in a table format.

* This is an edited, excerpted and augmented edition of a CRS Report RL33572, dated March 18, 2008 publication.

INTRODUCTION

With recent high energy prices and the passage of the Energy Policy Act of 2005 (P.L. 109-58) and the Energy Independence and Security Act of 2007 (P.L. 110-140), there is ongoing congressional interest in promoting greater use of alternatives to petroleum fuels. Biofuels — transportation fuels produced from plants and other organic materials — are of particular interest. Ethanol and biodiesel, the two most widely used biofuels, receive significant federal support in the form of tax incentives, loan and grant programs, and regulatory programs. [1] Further action on biofuels is likely as Congress negotiates on a Farm Bill in the 110th Congress. [2]

This report outlines 18 current and expired federal programs and provisions (plus one authorized but unfunded program) that provide direct or indirect incentives for biofuels. The programs are grouped below by administering agency. The incentives for biofuels are summarized in the Appendix. This information is compiled from authorizing statutes, committee reports, and Administration budget request documents.

ENVIRONMENTAL PROTECTION AGENCY (EPA)

Renewable Fuel Standard

Administered by: EPA Annual funding: N/A FY2008 budget request: N/A Established: 2005 by the Energy Policy Act of 2005, §1501 (P.L. 109-58); expanded by the Energy Independence and Security Act of 2007, §202 (P.L. 110-140) Scheduled termination: None Description: The Energy Policy Act of 2005 established a renewable fuels standard (RFS) for automotive fuels. The RFS was expanded bythe EnergyIndependence and Security Act of 2007. The RFS requires the blending of renewable fuels (including ethanol and biodiesel) in transportation fuel. [3] In 2008, fuel suppliers must blend 9.0 billion gallons of renewable fuel into gasoline; this requirement increases annually to 36 billion gallons in 2022. The expanded RFS also specifically mandates the use of "advanced biofuels" — fuels produced from non-corn feedstocks and with 50% lower lifecycle greenhouse gas emissions than petroleum fuel — starting in 2009. Of the 36 billion gallons required in 2022, at least 21 billion gallons must be advanced biofuel. There are also specific quotas for cellulosic biofuels and for biomass-based diesel fuel. On May 1, 2007, EPA issued a final rule on the RFS program detailing compliance standards for fuel suppliers, as well as a system to trade renewable fuel credits between suppliers. [4] While this program is not a direct incentive for the construction of biofuels plants, the guaranteed market created by the renewable fuel standard is expected to stimulate growth of the biofuels industry.

INTERNAL REVENUE SERVICE (IRS)

Volumetric Ethanol Excise Tax Credit

Administered by: Internal Revenue Service Annual funding: N/A Established: 2005 by the American Jobs Creation Act of 2004, §301 (P.L. 108-357) Scheduled termination: December 31, 2010 Description: Gasoline suppliers who blend ethanol with gasoline are eligible for a tax credit of 51 cents per gallon of ethanol. Qualified applicant: Blenders of gasohol (i.e., gasoline suppliers and marketers) For more information: IRS Publication 510, Chapter 2: Fuel Tax Credits and Refunds [http://www.irs.gov/publications/p510/ch02.html]

Small Ethanol Producer Credit

Administered by: Internal Revenue Service Annual funding: N/A Established:1990 by the Omnibus Budget Reconciliation Act of 1990, §11502 (P.L. 101-508); extended by the American Jobs Creation Act of 2004, §301 (P.L. 108357); expanded by the Energy Policy Act of 2005, §1347 (P.L. 109-58) Scheduled termination: December 31, 2010 Description: The small ethanol producer credit is valued at 10 cents per gallon of ethanol produced. The credit may be claimed on the first 15 million gallons of ethanol produced by a small producer in a given year. Qualified applicant: Any ethanol producer with production capacity below 60 million gallons per year For more information: IRS Publication 510, Chapter 2: Fuel Tax Credits and Refunds [http://www.irs.gov/publications/p510/ch02.html]

Biodiesel Tax Credit

Administered by: Internal Revenue Service Annual funding: N/A Established: 2005 by the American Jobs Creation Act of 2004, §302 (P.L. 108-357); extended by the Energy Policy Act of 2005, §1344 (P.L. 109-58) Scheduled termination: December 31, 2008 Description: Biodiesel producers (or producers of diesel/biodiesel blends) can claim a per-gallon tax credit. The credit is valued at $1.00 per gallon of "agri-biodiesel" (biodiesel produced from virgin agricultural products such as soybean oil or animal fats), or 50 cents per gallon of biodiesel produced from previously used agricultural products (e.g., recycled fryer grease). Qualified applicant: Biodiesel producers and blenders For more information: IRS Publication 510, Chapter 2: Fuel Tax Credits and Refunds [http://www.irs.gov/publications/p510/ch02.html]

Small Agri-Biodiesel Producer Credit

Administered by: Internal Revenue Service Annual funding: N/A Established: 2005 by the Energy Policy Act of 2005, §1345 (P.L. 109-58) Scheduled termination: December 31, 2008 Description: The small agri-biodiesel producer credit is valued at 10 cents per gallon of "agri-biodiesel" (see Biodiesel Tax Credit, above) produced. The credit may be claimed on the first 15 million gallons of ethanol produced by a small producer in a given year. Qualified applicant: Any agri-biodiesel producer with production capacity below 60 million gallons per year For more information: IRS Publication 510, Chapter 2: Fuel Tax Credits and Refunds [http://www.irs.gov/publications/p510/ch02.html]

Renewable Diesel Tax Credit

Administered by: Internal Revenue Service Annual funding: N/A Established: 2005 by the Energy Policy Act of 2005, §1346 (P.L. 109-58) Scheduled termination: December 31, 2008 Description: Producers of biomass-based diesel fuel made through a thermal depolymerization process (or producers of diesel/renewable biodiesel blends) can claim $1.00 per gallon tax credit. As defined by law, diesel fuel substitutes produced through thermal processes are not considered "biodiesel," and thus are ineligible for the biodiesel credits. Qualified applicant: Renewable diesel producers and blenders For more information: IRS Publication 510, Chapter 2: Fuel Tax Credits and Refunds [http://www.irs.gov/publications/p510/ch02.html]

Special Depreciation Allowance for Cellulosic Biomass

Ethanol Plant Property

Administered by: Internal Revenue Service Annual funding: N/A Established: 2006 by the Tax Relief and Health Care Act of 2006, §209 (P.L. 109432) Scheduled termination: December 31, 2012 Description: A taxpayer may take a depreciation deduction of 50% of the adjusted basis of a new cellulosic ethanol plant in the year it is put in service. The accelerated depreciation applies only to cellulosic ethanol plants that break down cellulose through enzymatic processes (as opposed to gasification). Any portion of the cost financed through tax-exempt bonds is exempted from the depreciation allowance. Qualified applicant: Any enzymatic cellulosic ethanol plant acquired after December 20, 2006, and placed in service before January 1, 2013. Any plant that had a binding contract for acquisition before December 20, 2006, does not qualify. For more information: See Senate Finance Committee, Summary of House-Senate Agreement on Tax, Trade, Health, and Other Provisions, December 7, 2006.

Department of Agriculture (USDA)

Bioenergy Program

Administered by: Commodity Credit Corporation (CCC) Annual funding: $100 million appropriated for FY2005, $60 million for FY2006; up to $150 million authorized annually for FY2004 through FY2006 FY2008 budget request: $0 Established: FY2001 in response to Executive Order 13134 (August 12, 1999) Developing and Promoting Biobased Products and Bioenergy, through CCC's general authority to conduct commodity programs; extended by the Farm Security and Rural Investment Act of 2002, §9010 (P.L. 101-171) Termination: End of FY2006 Description: The Bioenergy Program reimbursed ethanol and biodiesel producers for expanding their production capacity. Payments helped defray the purchase cost of the additional commodities needed for that expansion. The amount of each payment was based on the change in production capacity, as well as the number of applicants selected for funding. Eligible commodities included grain and oilseed crops (e.g. barley, corn, soybeans), cellulosic crops (e.g. switchgrass, rice hulls), animal fats, agricultural byproducts, and oils. Qualified applicant: Any ethanol or biodiesel producer who expanded production capacity

Renewable Energy Systems and Energy Efficiency Improvements

Administered by: Rural Business Cooperative Service *Annual funding:* $23 million for all projects through FY2007, including biofuels projects; $36 million for FY2008 *FY2008 budget request:* $34 million *Established:* FY2003 by the Farm Security and Rural Investment Act of 2002, §9006

(P.L. 101-171); funding authorization for FY2007 reduced to $3 million by §1301 of the Deficit Reduction Act of 2005 (P.L. 109-171); full funding restored by FY2007 Continuing Resolution (P.L. 110-5) *Scheduled termination:* End of FY2007 *Description:* This program provides grants, loans, and loan guarantees for the development of renewable energy projects and energy efficiency improvements. The construction of a biofuel plant could be an eligible project. Grants are limited to 25% of the costs of the project; loans are limited to 50% of the cost of the project. *Qualified applicant:* Farmers, ranchers, and rural small businesses *For more information:* [http://www.rurdev.usda.gov]

Value-Added Producer Grants Program (VAPG)

Administered by: Rural Business Cooperative Service Annual funding: $15.5 million appropriated for FY2005; $20.5 million for FY2006; $20.3 million for FY2007; $18.9 million for FY2008 FY2008 budget request: $15 million Established: FY2001, expanded in FY2003 to include renewable energy projects by the Farm Security and Rural Investment Act of 2002, §6401 (P.L. 101-171); the Deficit Reduction Act of 2005, §1402 (P.L. 109-171), required that all previously appropriated funds unobligated by October 1, 2006 be returned to the Treasury Scheduled termination: End of FY2007 Description: VAPG provides grants to independent producers for the development of value-added agricultural activities, including biofuel production. The grants can be used for feasibility studies, the development of a business plan, or to acquire working capital to operate a value-added business. Grants are limited to $500,000 per recipient. Qualified applicant: Independent producer, producer group, cooperative, or a majority-controlled producer-based business venture For more information: [http://www.rurdev.usda.gov/rbs/coops/vadg.htm]

Biorefinery Development Grants (Unfunded)

Administered by: If funded, it would likely be administered by USDA's Rural Development Agency Annual funding: $0 Established: 2002 by the Farm Security and Rural Investment Act of 2002, §9003 (P.L. 101-171) Scheduled termination: End of FY2007 Description: This program was established by the Farm Security and Rural Investment Act of 2002 (P.L. 101-171); however, no funding has been provided. If funded, the program would provide grants for the development and construction of biorefineries, including those that produce biofuels. Qualified applicant: Virtually any non-federal entity (including a national laboratory) or group of entities that plans to build a biorefinery For more information: N/A

Business and Industry (B&I) Guaranteed Loans

Administered by: Rural Business Cooperative Service Annual funding: Approximately $1 billion in loans are guaranteed annually Scheduled termination: None Description: This program provides guarantees for up to 90% of a loan made by a commercial lender. Loan proceeds may be used for working capital, machinery and equipment, buildings and real estate, and certain types of debt refinancing. Qualified applicant: Virtually any legal entity. For more information: [http://www.rurdev.usda.gov/rbs/busp/b&i_gar.htm]

Rural Business Enterprise Grants (RBEG)

Administered by: Rural Business Cooperative Service Annual funding: Approximately $40 million in each of FY2005 through FY2007; $38.7 million for FY2008 Scheduled termination: None Description: RBEG provides grants to finance and facilitate development of small and emerging private rural business enterprises. The grant is awarded to a third party to assist a business; grant funds do not go directly to the business. Qualified applicant: Public bodies, private nonprofit corporations, and federally recognized Indian Tribal groups. For more information: [http://www.rurdev.usda.gov/rbs/busp/rbeg.htm]

Other USDA Programs

The following programs within the Rural Business Cooperative Service could possibly be used to assist biofuels producers indirectly:

- Rural Economic Development Loan Program;
- Rural Development Loan Program;
- Rural Economic Development Grants.

DEPARTMENT OF ENERGY (DOE)

Biomass Research and Development Initiative

Administered by: National Biomass Coordination Office (a joint DOE-USDA program) Annual funding: $14 million per year through FY2007 ($12 million in FY2006); $11 million for FY2008 FY2008 budget request: $12 million Established: FY2001 by the Biomass Research and Development Act of 2000, §307 (P.L. 106-224); program extended and mandatory appropriations provided bythe Farm Security and Rural Investment Act of 2002, §9008 (P.L. 101-171); program extended and funding authorization expanded by the Energy Policy Act of 2005, §941 (P.L. 109-58) — currently authorized at $200 million per year Scheduled termination: End of FY2015 Description: Grants are provided for biomass research, development, and demonstration projects. Eligible projects include ethanol and biodiesel demonstration plants. Qualified applicant: Wide range of possible applicants For more information: [http://www.brdisolutions.com/default.aspx]

Biorefinery Project Grants

Administered by: Office of Energy Efficiency and Renewable Energy Annual funding: For FY2008, $186 million appropriated for the biomass program — not all of this funding will go toward biorefinery project grants FY2008 budget request: $179 million for entire biomass program Established: FY2001 through funding authorized in various statutes Scheduled termination: None Description: This program provides funds for cooperative biomass research and development for the production of fuels, electric power, chemicals, and other products. Qualified applicant: Varies from year to year, depending on program goals in a given year For more information: [http://www.eere.energy.gov/biomass/]

Loan Guarantees for Ethanol and Commercial Byproducts from Cellulose, Municipal Solid Waste, and Sugar Cane

Administered by: DOE Annual funding: Not specified FY2008 budget request: $0 Established: 2005 by the Energy Policy Act of 2005, §§1510, 1511, and 1516 (P.L 109-58) Scheduled termination: Varies, depending on specific program Description: The Energy Policy Act of 2005 authorizes several programs to provide loan guarantees for the construction of facilities that produce ethanol and other commercial products from cellulosic material, municipal solid waste, or sugar cane. Qualified applicant: Private lending institutions, to guarantee loans for the construction of biofuels plants

DOE Loan Guarantee Program

Administered by: DOE Annual funding: $5.3 million for administrative expenses; authority for $38.5 billion in loan guarantees for energy projects in FY2008, including $10 billion for renewable energy and energy efficiency FY2008 budget request: $2 million for administrative expenses Established: 2005 by the Energy Policy Act of 2005, Title XVII (P.L 109-58) Scheduled termination: Not specified Description: Title XVII of the Energy Policy Act of 2005 authorizes DOE to provide loan guarantees for energy projects that reduce air pollutant and greenhouse gas emissions, including biofuels projects.

Qualified applicant: Private lending institutions, to guarantee loans for clean energy projects.For more information: [http://www.lgprogram.energy.gov/]

Cellulosic Biofuels Production Incentive

Administered by: DOE Annual funding: $25 million total authorized for all fiscal years FY2008 budget request: None Established: 2005 by the Energy Policy Act of 2005, §942 (P.L 109-58) Scheduled termination: Not specified Description: Section 942 of the Energy Policy Act of 2005 authorizes DOE to provide per-gallon incentive payments for cellulosic biofuels until annual U.S. production reaches 1 billion gallons or 2015, whichever is earlier. DOE accepted comments on the program through July 14, 2006; DOE has yet to promulgate regulations. Qualified applicant: Any U.S. cellulosic biofuel production facility that meets applicable permitting requirements, as well as any financial requirements set by DOE.

U.S. Customs and Border Protection

Import Duty for Fuel Ethanol

Administered by: U.S. Customs and Border Protection Annual funding: N/A Established: 1980 by the Omnibus Reconciliation Act of 1980 (P.L. 96-499); amended by the Tax Reform Act of 1986, §423 (P.L. 99-514; extended by the Tax Relief and Health Care Act of 2006, §302 (P.L. 109-432). Scheduled termination: December 31, 2008 Description: A 2.5% ad valorem tariff and a most-favored-nation duty of $0.54 per gallon of ethanol (for fuel use) applies to imports into the United States from most countries; most ethanol from Caribbean Basin Initiative (CBI) countries may be imported duty-free. Covered Entities: Fuel ethanol importers For more information: CRS Report RS21930, Ethanol Imports and the Caribbean Basin Initiative, by Brent D. Yacobucci; Senate Finance Committee, Summary of House-Senate Agreement on Tax, Trade, Health, and Other Provisions, December 7, 2006.

Appendix. Summary of Federal Incentives for Promoting Biofuels

Table 1. Federal Biofuels Incentives by Agency

Administering Agency	Program	Description	Original Authorizing Legislation	FY2008 Funding	Expiration Date
Environmental Protection Agency	Renewable Fuels Standard	Mandated use of renewable fuel in gasoline: 4.0 billion gallons in 2006, increasing to 7.5 billion gallons in 2012	P.L. 109-58 §1501	N/A	None
Internal Revenue Service	Volumetric Ethanol Excise Tax Credit	Gasoline suppliers who blend ethanol with gasoline are eligible for a tax credit of 51 cents per gallon of ethanol	P.L. 108-357 §301	N/A	End of 2010
	Small Ethanol Producer Credit	An ethanol producer with less than 60 million gallons per year in production capacity may claim a credit of 10 cents per gallon on the first 15 million gallons produced in a year	P.L. 101-508	N/A	End of 2010
	Biodiesel Tax Credit	Producers of biodiesel or diesel/biodiesel blends may claim a tax credit of $1.00 per gallon of agri-biodiesel (produced from virgin agricultural products) or 50 cents per gallon of biodiesel from recycled products	P.L. 108-357	N/A	End of 2008
	Small Agri-Biodiesel Producer Credit	An agri-biodiesel producer (see above) with less than 60 million gallons per year in production capacity may claim a credit of 10 cents per gallon on the first 15 million gallons produced in a year	P.L. 109-58	N/A	End of 2008

Table 1. Federal Biofuels Incentives by Agency (Continued)

Administering Agency	Program	Description	Original Authorizing Legislation	FY2008 Funding	Expiration Date
	Renewable Diesel Tax Credit	Producers of renewable diesel (similar to biodiesel, but produced through a different process) may claim a tax credit of $1.00 per gallon.	P.L. 109-58	N/A	End of 2008
	Special Depreciation Allowance for Cellulosic Biomass Ethanol Plant Property	Plants producing cellulosic ethanol through enzymatic processes may take a 50% depreciation allowance in the first year of operation, subject to certain restrictions	P.L. 109-432	N/A	End of 2012
Department of Agriculture	Bioenergy Program	Reimburses ethanol and biodiesel producers for feedstocks necessary to expand operations	P.L. 101-171 §9010	$0	Expired: End of FY2006
	Renewable Energy Systems and Energy Efficiency Improvements	Grants, loans, and loan guarantees for the development of renewable energy projects and energy efficiency improvements	P.L. 101-171 §9006	$36 million	Scheduled: End of FY2007
	Value-Added Producer Grants	Grants to independent producers for the development of value-added agricultural activities, including biofuel production	P.L. 101-171 §6401	$19 million	Scheduled: End of FY2007
	Biorefinery Development Grants - Unfunded	If funded, would provide grants for the development and construction of biorefineries, including biofuel plants	P.L. 101-171 §9003	$0	Scheduled: End of FY2007
	Business and Industry (B&I) Guaranteed Loans	Loan guarantees for various projects — could be used for biofuels	Various statutes	Approx. $1 billion	None
	Rural Business Enterprise Grants	Grants to finance and facilitate development of small and emerging rural business enterprises	Various statutes	Approx. $40 million	None
Department of Energy	Biomass Research and Development Initiative	Grants for biomass research, development, and demonstration projects	P.L. 106-224	$11 million	End of FY2015

	Biorefinery Project Grants	Funds cooperative R&D on biomass for fuels, power, chemicals, and other products	Various statutes	$186 million total for biomass program R&D	None
Administering Agency	Program	Description	Original Authorizing Legislation	FY2008 Funding	Expiration Date
	Loan Guarantees for Ethanol and Commercial Byproducts from Various Feedstocks	Several programs of loan guarantees to construct facilities that produce ethanol and other commercial products from cellulosic material, municipal solid waste, and/or sugarcane	P.L. 109-58 §§1510, 1511, and 1516	N/A	Varies
	DOE Loan Guarantee Program	Loan guarantees for energy projects that reduce air pollutant and greenhouse gas emissions, including biofuels projects	P.L. 109-58 Title XVII	N/A	None
	Production Incentives for Cellulosic Biofuels	Authorizes DOE to provide per-gallon payments to cellulosic biofuel producers	P.L. 109-58 §942	N/A	August 8, 2015
U.S. Customs and Border Protection	Import Duty for Fuel Ethanol	All imported ethanol is subject to a 2.5% ad valorem tariff; fuel ethanol is also subject to a most-favored nation added duty of 54 cents per gallon (with some exceptions)	P.L. 96-499	N/A	End of 2008

REFERENCE

[1] For more information on ethanol, see CRS Report RL33290, Fuel Ethanol: Background and Public Policy Issues, by Brent D. Yacobucci. For more information on biofuels in general, see CRS Report RL30758, Alternative Transportation Fuels and Vehicles: Energy, Environment, and Development Issues, by Brent D. Yacobucci, and CRS Report RL32712, Agriculture-Based Renewable Energy Production, by Randy Schnepf.
[2] For more information on the Farm Bill, see CRS Report RL33934, Farm Bill Legislative Action in the 110th Congress, coordinated by Renée Johnson.
[3] The original requirement was for renewable fuel in gasoline. P.L. 110-140 expanded the mandate to include all transportation fuels, and increased the amount of renewable fuel mandated annually.
[4] 72 Federal Register 23899-24014.

In: Energy Policy: Issues, Actions and Consequences
Editors: Quentin V. Harris
ISBN 978-1-60692-225-5

Chapter 5

THE CARBON CYCLE: IMPLICATIONS FOR CLIMATE CHANGE AND CONGRESS*

Peter Folger

ABSTRACT

Carbon is stored in the atmosphere, in the oceans, in vegetation, and in soils on the land surface. Huge quantities of carbon are actively exchanged between the atmosphere and the other storage pools of carbon. The exchange, or flux, of carbon between the atmosphere, oceans, and land surface is called the carbon cycle. In sheer magnitude, human activities contribute a relatively small amount of carbon, primarily as carbon dioxide (CO_2), to the global carbon cycle. Burning fossil fuels, for example, adds less than 5% to the total amount of CO_2 released from the oceans and land surface to the atmosphere each year. If humans add only a small amount of CO_2 to the atmosphere each year, why is that contribution important to global climate change?

In short, the oceans, vegetation, and soils cannot consume carbon released from human activities quickly enough to stop CO_2 from accumulating in the atmosphere. Humans tap the huge pool of fossil carbon for energy, and affect the global carbon cycle by transferring fossil carbon — which took millions of years to accumulate — into the atmosphere over a relatively short time span. As a result, the atmosphere contains 100 parts per million more today (380 ppm vs 280 ppm) than prior to the beginning of the industrial revolution. As the CO_2 concentration grows it increases the *radiative forcing* (more incoming radiation energy than outgoing) of the atmosphere, warming the planet. In response, Congress is considering legislative strategies that would reduce U.S. emissions of CO_2, or increase the uptake of CO_2 from the atmosphere, or both.

Less than half of the total amount of CO_2 released from burning fossil fuels during the past 250 years has remained in the atmosphere because two huge reservoirs for carbon — the global oceans and the land surface — take up more carbon than they release. They are net *sinks* for carbon. If the oceans, vegetation, and soils did not accumulate as much carbon as they do today, then the concentration of CO_2 in the

---

* This is an edited, excerpted and augmented edition of a CRS Report RL34059, dated June 25, 2007 publication.

atmosphere would increase even more rapidly. A key issue to consider is whether these two sinks will continue to store carbon at the same rate over the next few decades. Will the sinks remove more, less, or the same amount of CO_2 released from fossil fuel combustion each year? Currently, most of the total global carbon sink is referred to as the *unmanaged*, or background, carbon cycle. Very little carbon is removed from the atmosphere and stored, or sequestered, by deliberate action.

Congress may opt to consider how land management practices, such as afforestation, conservation tillage, and other techniques, might increase the net flux of carbon from the atmosphere to the land surface. How the ocean sink could be managed to store more carbon is unclear. Iron fertilization and deep ocean injection of CO_2 are in an experimental stage, and their promise for long-term enhancement of carbon uptake by the oceans is not well understood. Congress may consider incorporating what is known about the carbon cycle into its legislative strategies, and may also evaluate whether the global carbon cycle is sufficiently well understood so that the consequences of long-term policies aimed at mitigating global climate change are fully appreciated.

INTRODUCTION

Congress is considering several legislative strategies that would reduce U.S. emissions of greenhouse gases — primarily carbon dioxide (CO_2) — or increase uptake and storage of CO_2 from the atmosphere, or both. Both approaches are viewed by many as critical to forestalling global climate changed caused, in part, by the buildup of greenhouse gases in the atmosphere from human activities. Others point out that the human contribution of carbon to the atmosphere is a small fraction of the total quantity of carbon that cycles back and forth each year between the atmosphere and two huge carbon reservoirs: (1) the global oceans, and (2) the land surface of the entire planet. The exchange, or flux, of carbon between the atmosphere, oceans, and land surface is called the global carbon cycle.

An understanding of the details of the global carbon cycle has shifted from being of mainly academic interest to being of political interest. Policy makers are grappling with, for example, the importance of recognizing carbon sequestration by forests; or determining under a greenhouse gas cap what level of carbon emissions would limit the concentration of atmospheric CO_2 to a specific value; or understanding the magnitude and timing of ocean acidification and its impact on marine life. In sheer magnitude, human activities contribute a relatively small amount of carbon, primarily as CO_2, to the global carbon cycle. Fossil fuel combustion, for example, adds less than 5% to the total amount of carbon released from the oceans and land surface to the atmosphere each year. If humans add only a small amount of CO_2 to the atmosphere, why is that contribution important enough to influence global climate change?

This report explores the answer to that question and attempts to put the human contribution of carbon to the atmosphere into the larger context of the global carbon cycle. The report focuses almost entirely on CO_2, although methane (CH_4), black carbon, and organic carbon pollution are also part of the carbon cycle and have roles in human-induced climate change. Carbon dioxide, alone, is responsible for over half of the change in Earth's radiation balance, and methane for about an additional 20%. [1]

Carbon Storage, Sources, and Sinks

Carbon is stored in the atmosphere, in the oceans, in vegetation, and in soils on the land surface. Carbon is actively exchanged (fluxes) between the atmosphere and the other storage pools, or stocks, of carbon. The atmosphere is also linked to fossil carbon in geological reservoirs — for example, oil, gas, and coal — via their extraction and combustion as fossil fuels. [2] Dissolved inorganic carbon in the ocean is the largest storage pool, followed in size by fossil carbon in geological reservoirs, and by the total amount of carbon contained in soils. The atmosphere itself contains nearly 800 billion metric tons of carbon [3] (or gigatonnes, GtC), which is more carbon than all of the Earth's living vegetation contains. [4] Table 1 and Figure 1 show the global amount of carbon held in storage in each pool that is linked to the atmosphere.

Carbon dioxide in the atmosphere has an average concentration around the globe of approximately 380 parts per million (ppm). [5] The atmosphere has a fairly uniform concentration of CO_2, although it shows minor variations (about 1%) by season — due to photosynthesis and respiration — and by latitude. [6] Carbon dioxide released from fossil fuel combustion mixes readily into the atmospheric carbon pool, where it undergoes exchanges with the ocean and land surface carbon pools. Thus, *where* fossil fuels are burned makes relatively little difference to the concentration of CO_2 in the atmosphere; emissions in any one region affect the concentration of CO_2 everywhere else in the atmosphere. [7]

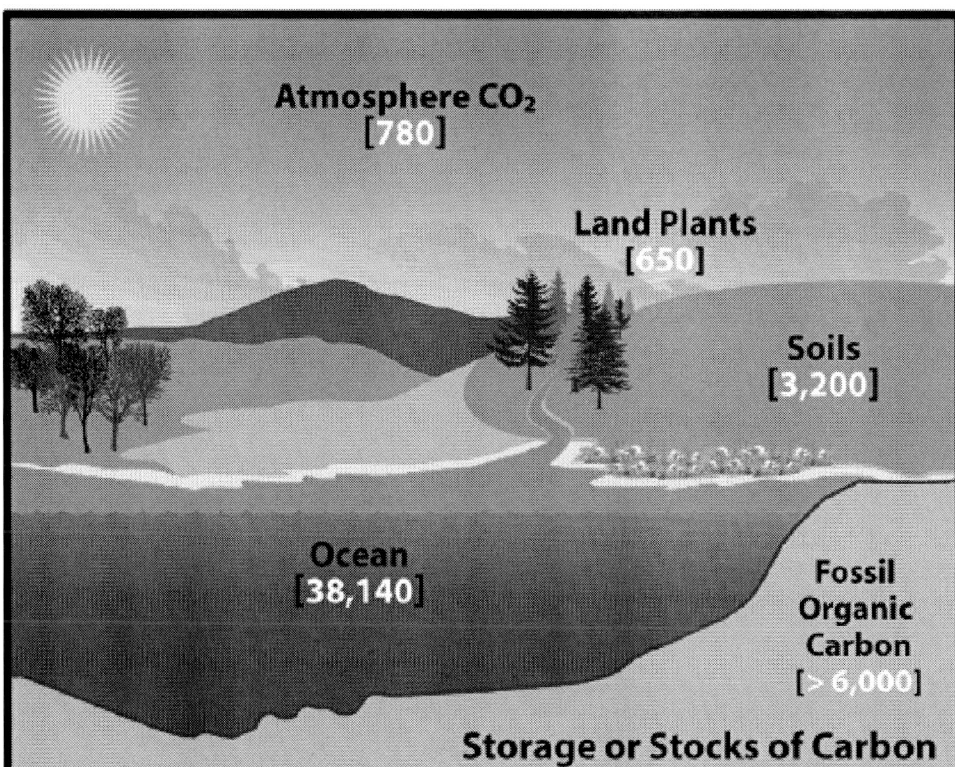

a.

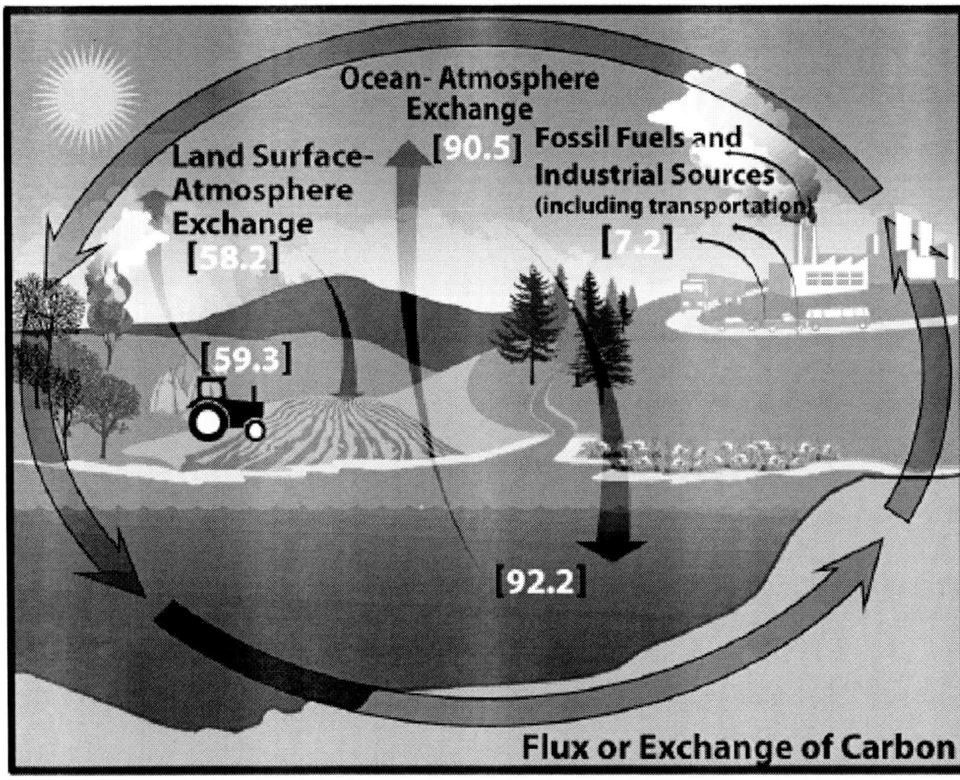

b.

Sources: SOCCR; IPCC Working Group I Report, Table 7.1; Sabine et al., "Current Status and Past Trends of the Global Carbon Cycle," in C.B. Field and M.R. Raupach (eds.), *The Global Carbon Cycle: Integrating Humans, Climate, and the Natural World*, Washington, D.C.: Island Press (2004), pp. 17-44. Note: Figure prepared by CRS.

Figure 1. (a) Storage or Stocks of Carbon (GtC); and (b) Annual Flux or Exchange of Carbon (GtC per year).

The oceans, vegetation, and soils truly exchange carbon with the atmosphere constantly on daily and seasonal time cycles. In contrast, carbon from fossil fuels is not exchanged with the atmosphere, but is transferred in a one-way direction from geologic storage, at least at the human time scale. [8] Some of the CO_2 currently in the atmosphere may become fossil fuel someday, after it is captured by vegetation, buried under heat and pressure, and converted into coal, for example, but the process takes millions of years. How much of the fossil fuel carbon ends up in the atmosphere, instead of the oceans, vegetation, and soils, and over what time scale, is driving much of today's global warming debate.

How much carbon is stored in each pool — especially the atmospheric pool — is important in the global warming debate because as more CO_2 is added to the atmosphere, its heat-trapping capacity becomes greater. [9] Each storage pool — oceans, soils, and vegetation — is considered a sink for carbon because each pool takes up carbon from the atmosphere. Conversely, each storage pool is also a source of carbon for the atmosphere, because of the constant exchange or flux between the atmosphere and the storage pools. The pool of fossil carbon is only a source, not a sink, except over geologic time scales, as described above. How much carbon is transferred between the atmosphere and the sources and sinks is a topic of scientific scrutiny because the mechanisms are still not understood completely. Whether a storage pool is a net sink or a net source for carbon in the future depends very much on the balance of mechanisms assumed to drive its behavior, and how those mechanisms may change. [10]

CARBON FLUX, OR EXCHANGE, WITH THE ATMOSPHERE

Over 90 billion tonnes (or 90 Gigatonnes of carbon, GtC) of carbon is exchanged each year between the atmosphere and the oceans, and close to 60 GtC is exchanged between the atmosphere and the land surface annually (Table 1). [11] Human activities — primarily land-use change and fossil fuel combustion — contribute less than 9 GtC to the atmosphere each year. [12] If the human contribution of CO_2 is removed from the equation, then the average net flux — the amount of CO_2 released to the atmosphere versus the amount taken up by the oceans, soils, and vegetation — is close to zero. Most scientists conclude that for 10,000 years prior to 1750, the net flux was less than 0.1 GtC per year when averaged over decades. [13] That small value for net flux is reflected by the relatively stable concentration of CO_2 in the atmosphere — between 260 and 280 ppm — for the past 10,000 years prior to 1750. [14]

Table 1. Carbon Stocks in the Atmosphere, Ocean, and Land Surface, and Annual Carbon Fluxes

Storage pool (or stock) in GtC			Annual flux (or exchange) *from the* atmosphere in GtC per year	Annual flux (or exchange) *to the* atmosphere in GtC per year	Net annual flux to the atmosphere in GtC per year
Atmosphere	780				
Ocean	38,140	Ocean-Atmosphereb	92.2	90.5	-1.7
Land Surfacea (soils plus vegetation)	3,850	Land Surface-Atmospherec	59.3	58.2	-1.1
Fossil Carbon (coal, gas oil, other)	>6,000	Fossil Carbon-Atmosphere	—	7.2	+7.2

Sources: SOCCR; IPCC Working Group I Report, Table 7.1; Sabine et al., "Current Status and Past Trends of the Global Carbon Cycle," in C.B. Field and M.R. Raupach (eds.), The Global Carbon Cycle: Integrating Humans, Climate, and the Natural World, Washington, D.C.: Island Press (2004), pp. 17-44. a The soil pool contains about 3,200 GtC, and the vegetation pool contains about 650 GtC. b Gross fluxes between the ocean and atmosphere have considerable uncertainty, but the net flux is known to within +/-0.3 GtC per year (SOCCR, p. 2-3). c The net flux between the land surface and the atmosphere is known to within +/-0.7 GtC per year (Jonathan A. Foley and Navin Ramankutty, "A Primer on the Terrestrial Carbon Cycle: What We Don't Know But Should," in C.B. Field and M.R. Raupach (eds.), The Global Carbon Cycle: Integrating Humans, Climate, and the Natural World, Washington, D.C.: Island Press (2004), p. 281.

Currently the atmospheric concentration of CO_2 is almost 100 ppm higher than it was before 1750 because human activities are adding carbon to the atmosphere faster than the oceans, land vegetation, and soils can remove it. The relatively rapid addition of CO_2 to the atmosphere has tipped the balance between sources and sinks. Why is that occurring?

The short answer is timing. First, the oceans and land surface are taking up carbon released from human activities, but not as quickly as CO_2 is accumulating in the atmosphere. About 45% of the CO_2 released from fossil fuel combustion and land use activities during the 1990s has remained in the atmosphere, while the remainder has been taken up by the oceans, vegetation, or soils on the land surface. [15] Carbon dioxide is nonreactive [16] in the atmosphere and has a relatively long residence time, although eventually most of it will return to the ocean and land sinks. About 50% of a single pulse of CO_2 will be removed within 30 years, a further 30% removed in within a few centuries, and the remaining 20% may persist in the atmosphere for thousands of years. [17] As the CO_2 concentration grows it increases the radiative forcing of the atmosphere, warming the planet. Second, the oceans and land surface are acting at present as sinks for CO_2 emitted from fossil fuel combustion and deforestation, but as they accumulate more carbon the nature of the sinks may change. It is also likely that climate change itself — for example, higher temperatures, more intense hydrologic cycle — may alter the balance between sources and sinks, due to changes in the complicated feedback mechanisms between the atmosphere, oceans, and land surface. [18] How carbon sinks will behave in the future is currently a prominent question for both scientists and policy makers.

Land Surface-Atmosphere Flux. Most estimates of the carbon cycle indicate that the land surface (vegetation plus soils) accumulates more carbon per year than it emits to the atmosphere (Figure 1 and Table 1). [19] The land surface thus acts as a net sink for CO_2 at present. Some policy makers advocate strategies for increasing the amount of CO_2 taken up and stored, or sequestered, by soils and plants, typically through agricultural or forestry practices. [20] How effective those strategies are likely to be depends, in part, on our understanding of the carbon cycle and the land-atmosphere flux.

The land use change component has the largest uncertainty of any component in the overall carbon cycle. [21] Most scientists agree, however, that in the past two decades tropical deforestation has been responsible for the largest share of CO_2 released to the atmosphere from land use changes. [22] Tropical deforestation and other land use changes may be responsible for releasing approximately 1.6 GtC per year to the atmosphere in the 1990s, and may be contributing similar amounts of carbon to the atmosphere today. [23] Even though deforestation releases more carbon than is captured by forest regrowth in some regions, net forest regrowth in other regions uptakes sufficient carbon so the land surface acts as a global net sink of approximately 1 GtC per year. By some estimates, even tropical lands, despite widespread deforestation, may be carbon-neutral or even net carbon sinks; tropical systems uptake substantial carbon to offset what is lost through deforestation. [24]

What used to be known as "the missing sink" component in the overall global carbon cycle is now understood to be that part of the terrestrial ecosystem responsible for the net uptake of carbon from the atmosphere to the land surface (especially high-latitude forests). [25] Scientists now prefer the term "residual land sink" to "missing sink" as it portrays the residual — or left over — part of the global carbon cycle calculation once the other components are accounted for (fossil fuel emissions, land-use emissions, atmospheric increase, and ocean uptake). [26] Precisely which mechanisms are responsible for the residual land sink are a topic of scientific controversy. One mechanism postulated for many years has been the fertilizing effect of increased atmospheric CO_2 concentrations on plant growth. Most models predict enhanced growth and carbon sequestration by plants in response to rising CO_2 levels; however, results of experiments have been mixed. Experiments show enhanced growth from increased CO_2 concentrations — at least initially — but nutrient availability and other limitations to growth are common. Long-term observations of biomass change and growth rates suggest that fertilization effects are too small to account for the residual land sink, at least in the United States. [27]

In North America, particularly the United States, the land-atmosphere flux is strongly tilted towards the land surface, where approximately 0.5 GtC per year is accumulating in terrestrial sinks. [28] That amount constitutes a large fraction — possibly 25% — of the global terrestrial carbon sink. [29] According to some estimates, approximately 50% of the North American terrestrial carbon sink stems from regrowth of forests on abandoned U.S. farmland. [30] Woody encroachment — the increase in woody biomass occurring mainly on former grazing lands — is thought to be another potentially large terrestrial sink, possibly accounting for 20% of the net North American sink (although the actual number is highly uncertain). [31] Wood products (e.g. furniture, house frames, etc.), wetlands, and other smaller, poorly understood carbon sinks are responsible for accumulating the remaining carbon in North America.

Most of the North American terrestrial carbon sink, such as the forest regrowth component, is sometimes referred to as the unmanaged, or background, carbon cycle. Very little carbon is sequestered by deliberate action. [32] The future behavior of the unmanaged terrestrial carbon sink is another consideration for lawmakers. Whether the United States will continue its trajectory as a major terrestrial carbon sink is highly uncertain, and some evidence suggests that the terrestrial ecosystem sinks may not increase in size. Some current sinks may even become sources for carbon. [33]

Policy makers may also need to evaluate how management practices, such as afforestation, conservation tillage, and other techniques would increase the net flux of carbon from the atmosphere to the land surface. [34] How forests, rangelands, and croplands are managed in the future for carbon sequestration may become an important factor in the overall land-atmosphere flux.

Ocean-Atmosphere Flux. Similar to the land surface, the oceans today accumulate more carbon than they emit to the atmosphere each year, acting as a net sink of about 1.7 GtC per year (Figure 1 and Table 1). If the land surface and oceans were not acting as net sinks, the CO_2 concentration in the atmosphere would be increasing at a faster rate than observed. More than the land surface, the oceans have a huge capacity to store carbon. Ultimately, the oceans could store more than 90% of all the carbon released to the atmosphere by human activities, but the process takes thousands of years. [35] Policy makers may be more concerned about how CO_2 is accumulating in the oceans now, what its impact is on ocean chemistry and marine life (e.g. ocean acidification), and how its behavior as a net sink may change over the next few decades.

Carbon dioxide enters the oceans by dissolving into seawater at the ocean surface, at a rate controlled by the difference in CO_2 concentration between the atmosphere and the sea surface. [36] Because the surface waters of the ocean have a relatively small volume — and thus a limited capacity to store CO_2 — how much CO_2 is stored in the oceans over the time scale of decades depends on ocean mixing and the transport of CO_2 from the surface to intermediate and deep waters. Mixing between surface waters and deeper portions of the ocean is a sluggish process; for example, the oldest ocean water in the world — found in the North Pacific — has been out of contact with the ocean surface for about 1,000 years. [37] Thus the slow rate of ocean mixing, and slow transport of CO_2 from the surface to the ocean depths, is of possible concern to policymakers because it influences the effectiveness of the ocean sink for CO_2, and because CO_2 added to the surface waters of the ocean increases its acidity.

In addition to the vertical mixing of the ocean, large-scale circulation of the oceans around the globe is a critical component for determining the effectiveness of the ocean sink. [38] Surface waters carrying anthropogenic CO2 descend into the ocean depths primarily in the North Atlantic and the Southern Oceans, part of the so-called oceanic “conveyor belt.” [39] Some model simulations suggest that the Southern Ocean around Antarctica accounts for nearly half of the net air-sea flux of anthropogenic carbon. [40] From that region, a large portion of dissolved CO_2 is transported north towards the subtropics. Despite its importance as a CO_2 sink, the Southern Ocean is poorly understood, and at least one study suggests that its capacity for absorbing carbon may be weakening. [41]

As CO_2 is added to the surface of the ocean from the atmosphere, it increases the acidity of the sea surface waters, with possible impacts to the biological production of organisms, such as corals. Corals, and calcifying phytoplankton and zooplankton, are susceptible to increased acidity as their ability to make shells in the water column is inhibited or possibly reversed, leading to dissolution. [42] Some reports indicate that sea surface pH has dropped by 0.1 pH units since the beginning of the industrial revolution. [43] One report suggests that pH levels could drop by 0.5 pH units by 2100, and suggests further that the magnitude of ocean acidification can be predicted with a high level of confidence. [44] The same report states, however, that research on the impacts of high concentrations of CO^2 on marine organisms is in its infancy.

The oceans appear to be a larger net sink for carbon than the land surface at present. As with the land surface, however, a consideration for policy makers is the future behavior of the ocean sink, particularly the Southern Ocean, given its importance to the net ocean-atmosphere CO_2 flux. In contrast to the terrestrial carbon sink, where management practices such as afforestation and conservation tillage may increase the amount of carbon uptake, it is unclear how the ocean carbon sink can be managed in a similar fashion. Some proposed techniques for increasing ocean sequestration of carbon, such as iron fertilization [45] and deep ocean injection of CO^2, are in an experimental phase and have unknown long-term environmental consequences. [46]

CONCLUSIONS

Huge amounts of carbon are exchanged between the atmosphere, the land surface, and the oceans each year. Humans are responsible for only a small fraction of the total exchange that, nonetheless, affects the global system by adding a large net flux of CO_2 to the atmosphere. Before the industrial revolution — and the large-scale combustion of fossil fuels, land-clearing and deforestation activities — the average net flux of CO_2 to the atmosphere hovered around zero for nearly 10,000 years. Because of the human contribution to the net flux, the amount of CO_2 in the atmosphere is now 100 ppm higher today than is has been for the past 10,000 years.

Congress is exploring legislative strategies that would alter the human component of the global carbon cycle. Strategies that limit emissions from fossil fuel combustion would reduce the current one-way transfer of fossil carbon to the atmosphere. What took millions of years to accumulate geologically is being released in only a few hundred years. Capturing CO_2 before it is released to the atmosphere and injecting it back into geological reservoirs — direct carbon sequestration — is one possible strategy to "short circuit" the geologic process and return the carbon underground over a human time scale. CO_2 injection into the subsurface has been used for decades to enhance recovery of oil; however, large-scale geologic sequestration of CO_2 for *storage* is currently in a pilot testing stage.

Less than half of the total amount of CO_2 released from burning fossil fuels over the past 250 years remains in the atmosphere, because two huge sinks for carbon — the global oceans and the land surface — take up more carbon than they release at present. Congress is exploring if and how management practices, such as afforestation, conservation tillage, and other techniques, might increase the net flux of carbon from the atmosphere to land surface. How the ocean sink could be managed to store more carbon is unclear. Iron fertilization and deep ocean injection of CO_2 are in an experimental stage, and their promise for long-term enhancement of carbon uptake by the oceans is not well understood.

Also of possible concern to Congress is how the ocean and land surface sinks will behave over the coming decades and longer, and whether they will continue to uptake more carbon than theyrelease. For example, carbon emissions may be capped so as to keep atmospheric CO_2 concentrations below a prescribed level at some future date, but changes in the magnitude, or even the direction, of the ocean or land-surface sinks may affect whether those target concentrations can be achieved. Congress may wish to incorporate what is known about the carbon cycle into its legislative strategies. Congress may also wish to evaluate whether the global carbon cycle is sufficiently well understood that the consequences of long-term policies aimed at mitigating global climate change are fully appreciated.

REFERENCE

[1] The First State of the Carbon Cycle Report (SOCCR): The North American Carbon Budget and Implications for the Global Carbon Cycle. Anthony W. King, Lisa Dilling, Gregory P. Zimmerman, David M. Fairman, Richard A. Houghton, Gregg Marland, Adam Z. Rose, and Thomas J. Wilbanks, eds., 2007. A report by the U.S. Climate Change Science Program (CCSP) and the Subcommittee on Global Change Research, Washington, DC; at [http://cdiac.ornl.gov/SOCCR/draft4.html]. (Hereafter referred to as SOCCR.) The SOCCR report is the fourth draft, and is not yet final. The Intergovernmental Panel on Climate Change, "Working Group I Contribution to the Fourth Assessment Report of the Intergovernmental Panel on Climate Change," Climate Change 2007: the Physical Science Basis (2007); at [http://ipcc-wg1.ucar.edu/wg1/wg1-report.html]. (Hereafter referred to as 2007 IPCC WG I Report.)

[2] Carbon in the Earth's crust is mainly in the form of carbonates, and is linked to the atmosphere by natural processes, such as erosion and weathering, and by metamorphism over geologic time scales. In contrast, the key source of fossil carbon for the purposes of this report are fossil fuels, which are now linked to the atmosphere almost entirely via human activities.

[3] One metric ton of carbon is equivalent to 3.67 metric tons of CO_2.

[4] William H. Schlesinger, Biogeochemistry: an Analysis of Global Change (2nd Ed.), San Diego, CA: Academic Press, (1997), p. 360. Hereafter referred to as Schlesinger, 1997.

[5] World Data Centre for Greenhouse Gases (WDCGG), WMO Greenhouse Gas Bulletin: The State of Greenhouse Gases in the Atmosphere Using Global Observations through 2005 (Geneva, 2006); at [http://gaw.kishou.go.jp/wdcgg.html].

[6] Schlesinger, 1997, p. 56.

[7] Concentrations of CO_2 are slightly higher in the northern hemisphere compared to the southern hemisphere, by several parts per million, because most of the emissions of CO_2 from human activities are in the north.

[8] An exception to this is the concept of direct carbon sequestration, or carbon capture and storage, whereby the geologic time scale cycle of carbon storage is "short circuited" by capturing CO_2 at its source — a fossil-fueled electricity generating plant for example — and injecting it underground into geologic reservoirs.

[9] See CRS Report RL33849, Climate Change: Science and Policy Implications, by Jane A. Leggett, for an explanation of the heat-trapping properties, or radiative forcing, of CO_2 and other greenhouse gases.

[10] Jorge L. Sarmiento and Nicolas Gruber, "Sinks for Anthropogenic Carbon," Physics Today (August, 2002), pp. 30-36.

[11] These massive exchanges of CO_2 between the atmosphere, oceans, and land surface result mostly from natural processes, such as photosynthesis, respiration, decay, and gas exchange between the ocean surface and the lower atmosphere.

[12] About 80% of human-related CO_2 emissions results from fossil fuel combustion, and 20% from land use change (primarily deforestation). Fossil fuel burning and cement production release approximately 7.2 GtC per year, land use change releases about 1.6 GtC per year (2007 IPCC Working Group I Report, pp. 501, 514-515).

[13] 2007 IPCC Working Group I Report, p. 514.

[14] Ice core data indicate that CO_2 concentrations ranged between 180 and 300 ppm over the past 650,000 years, and between 275 and 285 ppm from AD 1000 to AD 1750 (2007 IPCC Working Group I Report, p. 137 and p. 435). See also E.T. Sundquist and K. Visser, "The Geologic History of the Carbon Cycle," in Heinrich D. Holland and Karl K. Turekian (eds.), Treatise on Geochemistry, Amsterdam, Netherlands: Elsevier Ltd. (2004), p. 443.

[15] IPCC Working Group I Report, pp. 514-515.

[16] As opposed to other greenhouse gases, such as methane (CH_4), which reacts with OH to produce water and CH3; and nitrous oxide (NO_2), which is decomposed in the atmosphere by its reaction with ultraviolet light.

[17] IPCC Working Group I Report, p. 515.

[18] See CRS Report RL33849, Climate Change: Science and Policy Implications, by Jane A. Leggett, for more information on climate feedback mechanisms.

[19] IPCC Working Group I Report, p. 515.

[20] For more information on sequestration in the agricultural and forestry sectors, see CRS Report RL31432, Carbon Sequestration in Forests, by Ross W. Gorte, and CRS Report RL33898, Climate Change: The Role of the U.S. Agriculture Sector, by Renee Johnson.

[21] IPCC Working Group I Report, p.518.

[22] IPCC Working Group I Report, p. 517.

[23] Ibid, Table 7.1.

[24] Ibid, p. 522. However, SOCCR (p. ES-6) notes that rates of forest clearing in the tropics, including Mexico, exceed rates of recovery and concludes that tropical regions dominated by rainforests or other forest types are a net source of carbon to the atmosphere.

[25] However, a recent study indicate that the northern latitude forests uptake less carbon than previously estimated, and tropical forests uptake more. See Britton B. Stephens et al., "Weak northern and strong tropical land carbon uptake from vertical profiles of atmospheric CO_2," Science, Vol. 316 (22 June 2007): pp. 1732-1735.

[26] SOCCR, p. 2-6.

[27] Sarmiento and Gruber (2002), p. 31.

[28] SOCCR, p. ES-9. This includes fluxes to and from land vegetation and soils, and excludes emissions from fossil fuel combustion, cement manufacturing, and other industrial processes.

[29] Ibid, p. ES-5. However, SOCCR reports that the magnitude of the global terrestrial carbon sink is highly uncertain.

[30] Ibid.

[31] SOCCR, p. ES-9; IPCC Working Group I Report, p. 527.

[32] SOCCR, pp. 2-3, 2-8.

[33] Ibid, p. 2-9.

[34] For more information on agricultural and forestry practices and carbon management, see CRS Report RL34032, Environmental Services Markets: Farm Bill Proposals; CRS Report RL33898, Climate Change: the Role of the U.S. Agricultural Sector, by Renee Johnson; and CRS Report RL31432, Carbon Sequestration in Forests, by Ross W. Gorte.

[35] CO_2 forms carbonic acid when dissolved in water. Over time, the solid calcium carbonate ($CaCO_3$) on the seafloor will react with, or neutralize, much of the carbonic acid that entered the oceans as CO_2 from the atmosphere. See David Archer et al., "Dynamics of fossil fuel CO_2 neutralization by marine $CaCO_3$," Global Biogeochemical Cycles (June 1998), vol. 12, no. 2, pp. 259-276.

[36] SOCCR, p. 2-7. In addition to the relative difference in CO_2 concentration between atmosphere and ocean, the rate of CO_2 dissolution also depends on factors such as wave action, wind, and turbulence.

[37] Sarmiento and Gruber (2002), p. 31.

[38] SOCCR, p. 2-7.

[39] Sarmiento and Gruber (2002), p. 31.

[40] Ibid.

[41] Corinne Le Quere et al., "Saturation of the Southern Ocean CO_2 sink due to recent climate change," Science, Vo. 316 (22 June, 2007): pp. 1735-1737.

[42] IPCC Working Group I Report, p. 529.

[43] Ibid. pH is measure of the concentration of hydrogen ions in solution. A lower pH means an increase in acidity, or a higher concentration of hydrogen ions.

[44] Ken Caldeira et al., "Ocean acidification due to increasing atmospheric carbon dioxide," The Royal Society, Policy Document 12/05 (June 2005), 60 pages; at [http:// www.royalsoc. ac.uk/].

[45] The deliberate introduction of iron into the surface ocean to stimulate marine phytoplankton growth, which would increase carbon sequestration from the atmosphere via photosynthesis. The Southern Ocean, in particular, is deficient in iron as a nutrient such that the introduction of iron could stimulate phytoplankton growth. Several experiments have been conducted or are underway to further explore this process, for example, Stephane Blain, et al., "Effect of natural iron fertilization on carbon sequestration in the Southern Ocean," Nature (April 26, 2007), vol. 446, no. 7139, pp. 1070-1074.

[46] For more information about injection of CO_2 into the deep oceans, see CRS Report RL33801, Direct Carbon Sequestration: Capturing and Storing CO_2, by Peter Folger.

INDEX

D

E

F

O

P

T

U